KIM MARSHALL

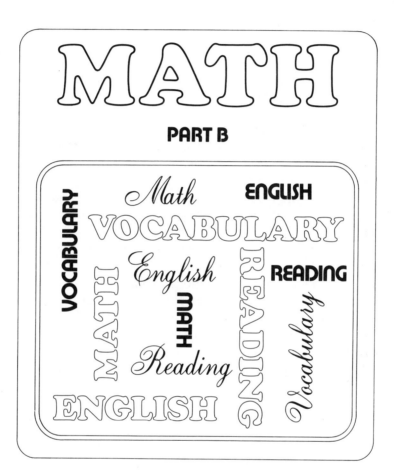

MATH

PART B

Educators Publishing Service, Inc.

Acknowledgments

Without the frank comments of my students in the Martin Luther King School in Boston, this book would not be what it is today. They gave me new insights every day, and they deserve much credit for the sequence, organization, content, and breakdown of the units in the book.

Rudd Crawford, a fellow teacher of math, is responsible for the idea of the cumulative review process, which he developed in a somewhat different form in his classroom in Brookline, Massachusetts. He is also responsible for Unit 9 on Adding and Subtracting Decimals. I am grateful to him, Mary Scott, and Ransom Lynch for their ideas, encouragement, and criticism over the years.

Jeff Rubin, an editor from Educators Publishing Service, played a major role in resequencing the units, eliminating unnecessary sections, revising the review pages, and expanding and rewriting the measurement units. His ideas have greatly improved the book.

I am grateful to these and other people for their substantive contributions, and to my wife, Rhoda Schneider, for her invaluable support over the last ten years.

Contents

To the Student

Math is divided into *Part A* and *Part B* and includes a total of thirty-five units. This book is *Part B* and should be introduced after *Part A.* However, if you already know the material in Review Test 18 in *Part A,* then you can begin with this book. The two books cover basic skills, Roman numerals, measurement, graphing, fractions, and basic geometry. If you work carefully through each unit, you should become a better math student and should be more confident in your ability to use math outside of school.

Each unit introduces one new skill. The sequence within each unit progresses as follows:

Page one and page two teach the new material.

Page three is a review with short practice questions on all the skills learned in previous units, so you won't forget them.

Page four and page five provide more practice on new material.

Page six is a test on the material learned in that unit.

Page seven is a Review Test which has one exercise that covers each skill introduced up to that point in the book.

The two-part box at the top of each page is your grade. The number already filled in is the number of questions on that page; the empty part of the box is for you or your teacher to write in the number you got right. At the back of the book is a progress chart where you can keep track of your grades on Unit Tests and on Review Tests. There is also a special bar graph on which to record your grades on these Review Tests. The top line of the bar graph indicates the level of one hundred percent correct on these Review Tests. The lower line represents an eighty percent level of achievement. You should try to keep your bar graph above the eighty percent line.

Good luck with these books. I hope you find them interesting and helpful.

KIM MARSHALL

Exponents are a short way of multiplying numbers by themselves. The little number written above the big one tells you how many times to write the big number and how many times to multiply it by itself. The little number is called the *exponent*.

Example:

3^2 means that you should write the 3 two times and multiply: $3 \times 3 = 9$.

5^3 means that you should write the 5 three times and multiply: $5 \times 5 \times 5 = 125$.

Different exponents are read in different ways. Examples of how to read and do exponents are given in the chart below.

Study the examples and then fill in the rest of the chart.

	Exponent	How you read it	How many times you multiply	Answer
	3^2	three squared	3×3	9
	3^3	three cubed	$3 \times 3 \times 3$	27
1.	3^4	three to the fourth		
2.	3^5	three to the fifth		
3.	3^6	three to the sixth		
4.	4^2			
5.	5^3			
6.	9^2			
7.	10^2			
8.	5^4			
9.	8^2			
10.	11^2			
11.	2^2			
12.	2^5			
13.	9^3			
14.	6^3			
15.	2^7			
16.	8^3			
17.	2^3			

Exponents 2

Remember:
  With a little ^{2} you say *squared*.
  With a little ^{3} you say *cubed*.
  With a little ^{4} you say to the *fourth*.
  With a little ^{5} you say to the *fifth*.

Fill in all of the chart below.

	Exponent	How you read it	How many times you multiply	Answer
1.	4^2			
2.	3^3			
3.	2^4			
4.	5^2			
5.	6^3			
6.	9^2			
7.	4^5			
8.	2^7			
9.		seven squared		
10.		two cubed		
11.		three to the sixth		
12.		twelve squared		
13.			8×8	
14.			$9 \times 9 \times 9$	
15.			$4 \times 4 \times 4 \times 4$	
16.			$7 \times 7 \times 7$	
17.			$2 \times 2 \times 2 \times 2 \times 2 \times 2$	
18.			$8 \times 8 \times 8$	
19.			$3 \times 3 \times 3 \times 3$	
20.				81
21.				9
22.				36

In each unit there will be a Review mixed in with the regular work pages. These Reviews are cumulative, so that they will give you the chance to practice what you learned in *Math — Part A* and all the things you learn in *Part B*. This way you won't forget the material.

Put the decimal in the right place in the answer to each problem below.

1. $93.1\overline{)596.771}$ 641

3. $.203\overline{)1.43318}$ 706

2. $619\overline{)466.726}$ 754

4. $.143\overline{)293.150}$ 2 050

Find the interval, and then figure out what *A* is on the following number lines.

5.
```
18        A                        54
 |_____|_____|_____|_____|
```

A = _____

6.
```
21        A
 |__|__|__|__|__|__|__|__|__|  30
```

A = _____

7. Factor 24 three ways. _____

_____ _____

8. Write 911,000,000,000,000 in words.

_____

9. 32297 ÷ 8 = _____

10. 4559.5 ÷ 5 = _____

11. Find the average of 12, 21, and 15.

_____

12. 23.7 − 14.631 = _____

13. 91.905 + 74.3 = _____

14. 21.7 × .45 = _____

15. Write four and eleven thousandths in numbers.

_____

16. Write 18.03 in words.

_____

17. Round off 47.83151 to the nearest one.

_____

18. 177.52 ÷ 2.8 = _____

19. Write MMCDXXXIV in Arabic numbers.

_____

20. A group of 5 friends went to the movies and spent $6.25 to get in. How much did each ticket cost?

_____

21. A toll collector at the end of the Pennsylvania Turnpike collects $1.35 from each car. How much will she get from 96 cars?

_____

22. Circle the best metric measure for measuring the weight of a horse.
    milligram
    gram
    kilogram

23. What is the best metric measure for measuring the weight of a grain of sugar?

_____

24. Circle the best metric measure for measuring the width of a postage stamp.
    millimeter
    centimeter
    meter
    kilometer

25. What is the best metric measure for measuring the length of a house?

_____

26. Circle the best metric measure for measuring the liquid in a can of soda.

   milliliter

   liter

27. What is the best metric measure for measuring the water in a bathtub?

   _____

28. How many days are in May? _____

29. How many days are in April? _____

30. How many quarts are in a gallon? _____

31. How many days are in a leap year? _____

32. How many quarters are in a dollar? _____

Exponents 3

Fill in all of the chart below.

	Exponent	How you read it	How many times you multiply	Answer
1.	9^3			
2.	4^4			
3.	10^2			
4.		three to the fifth		
5.		two to the eighth		
6.		six cubed		
7.			$2 \times 2 \times 2 \times 2$	
8.			$8 \times 8 \times 8$	
9.			$9 \times 9 \times 9$	
10.		twelve squared		
11.				49
12.				25
13.				64

Now work out the following problems. First work out each exponent; then add or subtract.

14. $2^2 + 4^2 =$ _____

15. $9^2 + 2^3 =$ _____

16. $5^3 + 6^2 =$ _____

17. $4^3 + 8^2 =$ _____

18. $2^4 - 3^2 =$ _____

5

Exponents 4

Fill in all of the chart below.

	Exponent	How you read it	How many times you multiply	Answer
1.	4^3			
2.		five squared		
3.	2^8			
4.			$3 \times 3 \times 3 \times 3$	
5.		nine cubed		
6.	6^2			
7.				100
8.			$5 \times 5 \times 5$	
9.	10^3			
10.		two to the fourth		

Now work out the following problems. First work out each exponent; then add or subtract.

11. $3^3 + 4^2 =$ _____

12. $12^2 - 2^3 =$ _____

13. $6^2 + 2^2 + 3^2 =$ _____

14. $2^5 - 1^9 =$ _____

15. $8^3 + 9^2 =$ _____

Use words to write each of the following numbers and exponents.

1. 4^3 _____

2. 8^2 _____

3. 5^4 _____

4. 6^7 _____

Write the following words as numbers with exponents. You don't have to work out the answers.

5. four squared = _____   6. nine cubed = _____   7. two to the fifth = _____

Work out the following problems.

8. 4^3 = _____

9. 6^3 = _____

10. 7^2 = _____

11. 4^4 = _____

12. 9^2 = _____

13. 2^5 = _____

14. 8^3 = _____

15. nine squared + five cubed = _____

16. six cubed + four squared = _____

17. $8^2 + 7^2$ = _____

18. $3^4 + 2^3$ = _____

19. $10^2 + 12^2$ = _____

20. $2^6 + 10^3$ = _____

Since this is *Math — Part B*, this Review Test is the sixteenth out of thirty-two tests which appear at the end of each unit. The tests go over the skills you have learned in previous weeks. The idea is to test you on new skills as you learn them and also to give you practice on the old ones. This way, by the end of the year, you should be good at all the skills you've learned and practiced in *Part A* and *Part B*.

Each skill will always be the same question number; for instance, question two will always be on writing numbers as words. As the tests get longer during the year, you will find the questions at the beginning easier and easier because you will have practiced them so much. If you do get a question wrong, be sure to check it over and understand your mistake. That way you will get it right on the next test you take.

1. Find the interval, and then figure out what *A* is on the following number line.

```
19            A            23
 |     |      |      |      |
```

A = _____

2. Write 305,000 in words.

_____

Write twenty-seven billion in numbers.

_____

3. Factor 24 three ways. _____

_____   _____

4. 24778 ÷ 8 = _____

5. Find the average of 17, 23, 46, and 30.

_____

6. Write 7.017 in words.

_____

Write two and seven hundredths in decimals.

_____

7. 35 + 8.91 + 7.397 = _____

8. 125.4 − 67.157 = _____

9. Round off 35,568,241 to the nearest million.

_____

10. Round off .4287459 to the nearest tenth.

_____

11. 6.49 × 5.7 = _____

12. Write MMCDLXXIV as an Arabic number.

_____

Write 3,721 in Roman numerals.

_____

13. 224.70 ÷ 3.5 = _____

A *fraction* is part of a whole thing, like $\frac{1}{2}$ a pie or $\frac{3}{4}$ of a dollar. The top number (the *numerator*) tells how many pieces you have. The bottom number (the *denominator*) tells how many pieces there are in one whole thing if it is divided into parts.

Put fractions next to each circle or square below. Make your fraction show the number of shaded parts over the total number of parts in each circle or square.

Example:

 = $\frac{1}{2}$

4. = ___

8. 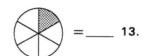 = ___

12.  = ___

1. = ___

5. = ___

9.  = ___

13.  : ___

2. = ___

6. = ___

10.  = ___

14.  = ___

3. = ___

7. = ___

11. 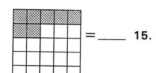 = ___

15. 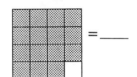 = ___

16. Which of the above fractions is equal to one whole? _____

17. Circle the following fractions which are equal to one whole.

$\frac{5}{6}$ $\frac{7}{7}$ $\frac{8}{11}$ $\frac{2}{3}$ $\frac{6}{6}$ $\frac{9}{9}$ $\frac{5}{7}$

If the denominators (bottoms) are the same, adding and subtracting fractions is easy. Just leave the denominator the same and add or subtract the numerators (tops).

Try the following problems.

Example:

$\frac{3}{8} + \frac{2}{8} = \frac{5}{8}$

21. $\frac{3}{9} + \frac{4}{9} = $ ——

25. $\frac{9}{14} + \frac{4}{14} = $ ——

18. $\frac{9}{10} - \frac{5}{10} = \frac{}{10}$

22. $\frac{5}{6} - \frac{4}{6} = $ ——

26. $\frac{2}{13} - \frac{1}{13} = $ ——

19. $\frac{6}{11} + \frac{4}{11} = $ ——

23. $\frac{4}{8} + \frac{3}{8} = $ ——

27. $\frac{7}{8} - \frac{5}{8} = $ ——

20. $\frac{2}{3} - \frac{1}{3} = $ ——

24. $\frac{2}{7} + \frac{5}{7} = $ ——

28. $\frac{6}{19} + \frac{4}{19} = $ ——

29. Which of the answers above is equal to one whole? _____

Next to each circle, write the fraction that shows the number of shaded parts and the total number of parts in that circle.

Example:

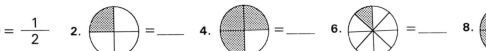

10. Which three of the fractions above are equal to one whole? _____ _____ _____

Now shade in the following circles. Look at the fractions to decide how many parts to shade in.

11. $\frac{1}{2}$ 15. $\frac{2}{2}$ 19. $\frac{1}{3}$ 23. $\frac{2}{3}$ 27. $\frac{3}{3}$

12. $\frac{1}{4}$ 16. $\frac{2}{4}$ 20. $\frac{3}{4}$ 24. $\frac{4}{4}$ 28. $\frac{1}{6}$

13. $\frac{2}{6}$ 17. $\frac{3}{6}$ 21. $\frac{4}{6}$ 25. $\frac{5}{6}$ 29. $\frac{6}{6}$

14. $\frac{1}{8}$ 18. $\frac{2}{8}$ 22. $\frac{3}{8}$ 26. $\frac{4}{8}$ 30. $\frac{8}{8}$

31. Which of the fractions above are equal to one whole?

_____ _____ _____ _____ _____

Now work out the following problems. Remember to leave the denominators the same.

32. $\frac{3}{4} - \frac{2}{4} =$ _____   34. $\frac{2}{11} + \frac{5}{11} =$ ____   36. $\frac{6}{8} + \frac{1}{8} =$ _____   38. $\frac{2}{3} + \frac{1}{3} =$ _____

33. $\frac{4}{8} - \frac{3}{8} =$ _____   35. $\frac{6}{7} - \frac{4}{7} =$ _____   37. $\frac{9}{10} - \frac{5}{10} =$ ____   39. $\frac{2}{13} + \frac{7}{13} =$ ____

Write the following words as numbers with exponents.

1. two squared _____

2. three squared _____

3. four cubed _____

4. five to the fourth _____

5. ten squared _____

6. nine to the sixteenth _____

Work out the following problems.

7. 3^2 = _____

8. 4^3 = _____

9. 9^2 = _____

10. 10^3 = _____

11. 2^5 = _____

Write the following numbers with exponents as words.

12. 5^3 _____

13. 6^5 _____

14. 7^3 _____

15. Figure out what A is on the following number line.

A = _____

16. Write 914,000,000,000 in words.

_____

17. Factors of 36 = _____

_____ _____

18. 63238 ÷ 7 = _____

19. Find the average of 118, 320, 214, and 400.

_____

20. Write two and seven tenths in decimals.

_____

21. Write 7.013 in words.

_____

22. 9 + 1.8 + 37.931 = _____

23. 6.3 − 1.471 = _____

24. Round off 65,521,318 to the nearest million.

_____

25. Round off 69.73148 to the nearest one.

_____

26. 149 × .49 = _____

27. Write MMCDXXII in Arabic numbers.

_____

28. Write 1,693 in Roman numerals.

_____

29. 41.663 ÷ .61 = _____

30. A car weighs 1.9 tons. How many pounds is that?

_____

31. Mungo Hulk weighs 845 pounds. He wants to lose 3 pounds every day of the month of March, and he plans to do it by starving himself and sweating in a Turkish bath. How much will he weigh at the end of March if he sticks to his plan?

_____

32. Circle the metric measure you would use to measure the length of a baseball bat.
    millimeter
    centimeter
    meter
    kilometer

33. Which metric measure would you use to measure the width of this book?

    _____

34. How many seconds are in a minute? _____

35. How many days are in a year? _____

36. How many ounces are in a pound? _____

37. How many years are in a century? _____

38. How many years are in a decade? _____

Shade in the following circles. Look at the fractions to decide how many parts to shade in.

1. $\frac{1}{2}$

3. $\frac{1}{4}$

5. $\frac{3}{4}$

7. $\frac{1}{3}$

9. $\frac{2}{3}$

2. $\frac{1}{6}$

4. $\frac{5}{6}$

6. $\frac{1}{8}$

8. $\frac{4}{8}$

10. $\frac{7}{8}$

Now work out the following problems.

11. $\frac{5}{6} - \frac{4}{6} =$ _____

12. $\frac{2}{3} + \frac{1}{3} =$ _____

13. $\frac{6}{11} + \frac{4}{11} =$ _____

14. $\frac{2}{5} + \frac{2}{5} =$ _____

15. $\frac{6}{9} - \frac{5}{9} =$ _____

16. $\frac{3}{8} + \frac{4}{8} =$ _____

17. $\frac{2}{7} + \frac{5}{7} =$ _____

18. $\frac{9}{10} - \frac{1}{10} =$ _____

19. $\frac{6}{9} - \frac{4}{9} =$ _____

20. $\frac{7}{8} + \frac{1}{8} =$ _____

21. $\frac{2}{13} + \frac{9}{13} =$ _____

22. $\frac{6}{7} - \frac{5}{7} =$ _____

23. $\frac{4}{5} - \frac{3}{5} =$ _____

24. $\frac{2}{9} + \frac{7}{9} =$ _____

25. $\frac{6}{10} + \frac{3}{10} =$ _____

26. $\frac{4}{17} + \frac{8}{17} =$ _____

27. Which of the answers above are equal to one whole? _____ _____ _____ _____

The following fractions are equal to one whole: $\frac{2}{2}$, $\frac{3}{3}$, $\frac{4}{4}$, $\frac{5}{5}$, $\frac{6}{6}$, and so on. You will need to use fractions which equal one whole in the problems below.
Remember: The denominator (bottom) of each fraction tells how many pieces there are in one whole thing if it is divided into parts.

Work out the following problems.

28. A boy eats $\frac{1}{3}$ of a pie. What fraction is left? _____$\overline{3}$_____

29. The boy eats $\frac{1}{4}$ of the pie. What fraction is left? _____

30. The boy eats $\frac{5}{8}$ of the pie. What fraction is left? _____

31. A girl got $\frac{9}{10}$ right on a test. What fraction did she get wrong? _____

32. If she got $\frac{7}{10}$ right, what fraction did she get wrong? _____

Shade in the following circles. Look at the fractions to decide how many parts to shade in.

1. $\frac{1}{4}$ 2. $\frac{3}{4}$ 5. $\frac{5}{8}$ 7. $\frac{7}{8}$ 9. $\frac{2}{3}$

2. $\frac{1}{2}$ 4. $\frac{1}{3}$ 6. $\frac{5}{6}$ 8. $\frac{1}{6}$ 10. $\frac{4}{4}$

Now work out the following problems.

11. $\frac{7}{9} - \frac{4}{9} = $ _____

12. $\frac{4}{5} - \frac{3}{5} = $ _____

13. $\frac{5}{8} + \frac{3}{8} = $ _____

14. $\frac{6}{12} + \frac{5}{12} = $ _____

15. $\frac{2}{11} + \frac{9}{11} = $ _____

16. $\frac{4}{9} + \frac{3}{9} = $ _____

17. $\frac{2}{8} + \frac{5}{8} = $ _____

18. $\frac{2}{3} + \frac{1}{3} = $ _____

19. $\frac{4}{13} + \frac{9}{13} = $ _____

20. $\frac{2}{17} - \frac{1}{17} = $ _____

21. $\frac{4}{9} + \frac{3}{9} = $ _____

22. $\frac{2}{7} + \frac{5}{7} = $ _____

23. $\frac{5}{10} + \frac{4}{10} = $ _____

24. $\frac{6}{7} - \frac{4}{7} = $ _____

25. $\frac{8}{9} - \frac{6}{9} = $ _____

26. $\frac{2}{21} + \frac{9}{21} = $ _____

27. Which of the answers above are equal to one whole?

_____ _____ _____ _____ _____

Now work out the following problems.

28. A hotel has $\frac{14}{20}$ of its rooms filled. What fraction of the hotel is not filled? _____

29. A boy gets $\frac{11}{25}$ right on a test. What fraction is wrong? _____

30. A girl eats $\frac{7}{8}$ of a pie. What fraction is left? _____

31. A used car salesman sells $\frac{24}{27}$ of his cars. What fraction is left? _____

32. $\frac{19}{24}$ of a class is present. What fraction of the class is not present? _____

33. $\frac{14}{21}$ of a class is girls. What fraction is boys? _____

34. $\frac{6}{26}$ of the alphabet is vowels. What fraction is consonants? _____

Shade in the correct number of parts in each circle below.

1. $\dfrac{1}{2}$

3. $\dfrac{3}{4}$

5. $\dfrac{1}{4}$

7. $\dfrac{1}{3}$

9. $\dfrac{2}{3}$

2. $\dfrac{5}{6}$

4. $\dfrac{1}{8}$

6. $\dfrac{3}{8}$

8. $\dfrac{7}{8}$

10. $\dfrac{1}{6}$

Now work out the following problems.

11. $\dfrac{4}{5} - \dfrac{3}{5} = $ _____

13. $\dfrac{9}{17} + \dfrac{7}{17} = $ ____

15. $\dfrac{5}{8} - \dfrac{4}{8} = $ _____

17. $\dfrac{6}{7} + \dfrac{1}{7} = $ _____

12. $\dfrac{4}{19} + \dfrac{8}{19} = $ ____

14. $\dfrac{3}{9} - \dfrac{2}{9} = $ _____

16. $\dfrac{6}{11} + \dfrac{5}{11} = $ ____

18. $\dfrac{5}{10} + \dfrac{4}{10} = $ ____

19. Which of the above answers are equal to one whole? _____ _____

Now work out the following problems.

20. A boy eats $\dfrac{3}{5}$ of a pie. What fraction of the pie is left? _____

21. A girl gets $\dfrac{2}{25}$ of a test wrong. What fraction is right? _____

22. A boy spends $\dfrac{51}{100}$ of a dollar on candy. What fraction of the dollar is left? _____

23. A car travels $\dfrac{13}{30}$ of a trip. What fraction of the trip is left to go? _____

24. A school is $\dfrac{97}{200}$ boys. What fraction of the school is girls? _____

1. Figure out what *A* is on the following number line.

```
16              A            48
 |   |   |   |   |   |   |   |
```

A = _____

2. Write 309,000,000,000 in words.

_____

Write four hundred ninety-seven million in numbers.

_____

3. Factor 18 in two ways.   _____

_____

4. $45523 \div 7 =$ _____

5. Find the average of 18, 36, and 24.

_____

6. Write 2.07 in words.

_____

Write eight and eleven thousandths in decimals.

_____

7. $3.5 + 21 + 2.479 =$ _____

8. $93.4 - 56.218 =$ _____

9. Round off 57,245 to the nearest thousand.

_____

10. Round off 73.7489213 to the nearest one.

_____

11. $2.07 \times .93 =$ _____

12. Write CMLXXXVI as an Arabic number.

_____

Write 2,742 in Roman numerals.

_____

13. $352.83 \div 5.7 =$ _____

14. Three squared + two cubed = _____

$5^4 =$ _____

Draw a line between each pair of fractions that is the same. Looking at the shaded parts will help you.

$\dfrac{1}{2}$ $\dfrac{2}{12}$

1. $\dfrac{1}{4}$ $\dfrac{4}{4}$

2. $\dfrac{3}{4}$ $\dfrac{2}{6}$

3. $\dfrac{2}{2}$ $\dfrac{2}{4}$

4. $\dfrac{1}{6}$ $\dfrac{2}{8}$

5. $\dfrac{1}{3}$ $\dfrac{4}{6}$

6. $\dfrac{2}{3}$ $\dfrac{6}{8}$

Shade in the second circle so it is equal to the first one. Then fill in the numerator (top) of the fraction next to the second circle and on the next line of the problem.

7. $\dfrac{1}{2}$ is the same as (is equivalent to) $\dfrac{}{4}$,

so $\dfrac{1}{2} = \dfrac{}{4}$

8. $\dfrac{1}{2}$ is the same as $\dfrac{}{8}$,

so $\dfrac{1}{2} = \dfrac{}{8}$

9. $\dfrac{1}{2}$ is the same as $\dfrac{}{6}$,

so $\dfrac{1}{2} = \dfrac{}{6}$

10. $\dfrac{2}{3}$ is the same as $\dfrac{}{6}$,

so $\dfrac{2}{3} = \dfrac{}{6}$

11. $\dfrac{3}{4}$ is the same as $\dfrac{}{8}$,

so $\dfrac{3}{4} = \dfrac{}{8}$

You can't always use drawings to find *equivalent fractions*. There is a quicker and easier way. Find the number that is multiplied by the old denominator (bottom) to get the new denominator; then multiply the old numerator (top) by the same number.

Solve the problems below. You will be finding equivalent fractions. An example has been done for you. Study it before you do the problems.

Example:

$$\dfrac{2}{3} \overset{\times 2}{\underset{\times 2}{=}} \dfrac{4}{6}$$

12. $\dfrac{4}{5} = \dfrac{}{10}$

13. $\dfrac{3}{5} = \dfrac{}{15}$

14. $\dfrac{6}{7} = \dfrac{}{21}$

15. $\dfrac{1}{3} = \dfrac{}{12}$

16. $\dfrac{6}{7} = \dfrac{}{14}$

17. $\dfrac{2}{3} = \dfrac{}{9}$

18. $\dfrac{4}{5} = \dfrac{}{20}$

19. $\dfrac{8}{9} = \dfrac{}{27}$

20. $\dfrac{1}{2} = \dfrac{}{12}$

21. $\dfrac{4}{7} = \dfrac{}{35}$

In each problem, shade in the circles so they are equal. Then fill in the numerator (top) of the fraction next to the second circle.

Find equivalent fractions. Remember to multiply or divide the numerator and denominator by the same number. Before you try the following problems, study the two examples which have been done for you.

1. $\frac{1}{2}$ 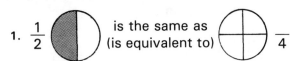 is the same as (is equivalent to) $\frac{}{4}$

Examples:

$$\frac{2}{3} \overset{\times 3}{\underset{\times 3}{=}} \frac{6}{9} \qquad \frac{14}{21} \overset{\div 7}{\underset{\div 7}{=}} \frac{2}{3}$$

2. $\frac{1}{2}$ is the same as $\frac{}{8}$

10. $\frac{4}{5} \underset{\times 2}{=} \frac{}{10}$

17. $\frac{8}{14} \underset{\div 2}{=} \frac{}{7}$

3. $\frac{1}{2}$ is the same as $\frac{}{6}$

11. $\frac{6}{7} = \frac{}{14}$

18. $\frac{12}{20} = \frac{}{5}$

4. $\frac{1}{2}$ is the same as $\frac{}{12}$

12. $\frac{1}{2} = \frac{}{8}$

19. $\frac{12}{27} = \frac{}{9}$

5. $\frac{1}{4}$ is the same as $\frac{}{8}$

13. $\frac{3}{7} = \frac{}{21}$

20. $\frac{12}{22} = \frac{}{11}$

6. $\frac{3}{4}$ is the same as $\frac{}{8}$

14. $\frac{4}{5} = \frac{}{20}$

21. $\frac{25}{45} = \frac{}{9}$

7. $\frac{4}{4}$ is the same as $\frac{}{8}$

15. $\frac{1}{9} = \frac{}{18}$

22. $\frac{20}{30} = \frac{}{3}$

8. $\frac{1}{3}$ is the same as $\frac{}{6}$

16. $\frac{3}{7} = \frac{}{42}$

23. $\frac{15}{50} = \frac{}{10}$

9. $\frac{2}{3}$ is the same as $\frac{}{6}$

In each drawing below, tell what fraction is shaded in.

1. _____

2. _____

3. _____

4. If $\frac{9}{10}$ of a test is right, what fraction is wrong?

_____

5. If $\frac{7}{15}$ of a job is done, what fraction remains to be done?

_____

6. If a tree is $\frac{4}{5}$ dead, what fraction is alive?

_____

7. $\frac{4}{7} + \frac{2}{7} =$ _____

8. $\frac{1}{11} + \frac{4}{11} =$ _____

9. $\frac{9}{10} + \frac{1}{10} =$ _____

10. Figure out what A is on the following number line.

```
14                        A        42
 |     |        |        |        |
```

A = _____

11. Factors of 27 = _____

12. Write four hundred seventeen billion in numbers.

_____

13. $7483 \div 6 =$ _____

14. Find the average of 17 and 31.

_____

15. Write 10.03 in words.

_____

16. $18.6 + 9.73 =$ _____

17. $93.4 - 19.138 =$ _____

18. Round off 16,793,211 to the nearest million.

_____

19. Round off 7.43799 to the nearest tenth.

_____

20. $14.9 \times 28 =$ _____

21. Write MMCDLXXVI in Arabic numbers.

_____

22. Write 3,624 in Roman numerals.

_____

23. Circle the measures for volume.
    kilometers
    liters
    feet
    cups
    gallons
    miles
    quarts
    milliliters
    meters

24. $40.992 - .61 =$ _____

25. $9^3 =$ _____

26. The fuel tank of Mr. Cante's car holds 15.4 gallons. How far can he drive on a full tank if the car gets 19 miles to each gallon?

_____

27. Jose broke open his piggy bank and found 15 quarters, 29 dimes, 37 nickels, and 215 pennies. How much is this in dollars and cents?

_____

28. How many days are in June? _____

29. How many days are in September? _____

30. How many days are in July? _____

31. How many days are in a leap year? _____

32. How many pounds are in a ton? _____

Write the equivalent fractions in the problems below.

1. $\dfrac{1}{2} = \dfrac{}{6}$

2. $\dfrac{3}{4} = \dfrac{}{12}$

3. $\dfrac{5}{6} = \dfrac{}{12}$

4. $\dfrac{8}{11} = \dfrac{}{33}$

5. $\dfrac{20}{25} = \dfrac{}{5}$

6. $\dfrac{2}{9} = \dfrac{}{18}$

7. $\dfrac{18}{21} = \dfrac{}{7}$

8. $\dfrac{1}{10} = \dfrac{}{30}$

9. $\dfrac{35}{49} = \dfrac{}{7}$

10. $\dfrac{2}{3} = \dfrac{}{33}$

11. $\dfrac{27}{30} = \dfrac{}{10}$

12. $\dfrac{1}{8} = \dfrac{}{40}$

If you are asked to find the *least common denominator,* you must give the same denominator to all the fractions you are working with. To find the least common denominator, you find the smallest number into which all denominators can be divided evenly.

Example:

$\dfrac{2}{3} = \dfrac{}{12}$ 3 and 4 can also be divided into 24, but 24 is not the least common denominator.

12 is the least common denominator for 3 and 4.

$\dfrac{3}{4} = \dfrac{}{12}$

Now find the least common denominators for the problems below. Make sure you write the least common denominators every place where they should be.

13. $\dfrac{5}{8} = $ _____   6 and 8 can both be divided into _____, so _____ is the common denominator.

$\dfrac{1}{6} = $ _____   Is it the lowest? _____

14. $\dfrac{1}{5} = $ _____   5 and 4 both go into _____, so _____ is the common denominator.

$\dfrac{3}{4} = $ _____   Is it the lowest? _____

15. $\dfrac{5}{6} = $ _____

$\dfrac{2}{3} = $ _____

16. $\dfrac{3}{10} = $ _____

$\dfrac{5}{6} = $ _____

Find the equivalent fractions in the following problems.

1. $\dfrac{2}{3} = \dfrac{}{9}$ 5. $\dfrac{8}{12} = \dfrac{}{3}$ 9. $\dfrac{5}{8} = \dfrac{}{24}$ 13. $\dfrac{1}{12} = \dfrac{}{36}$

2. $\dfrac{15}{18} = \dfrac{}{6}$ 6. $\dfrac{18}{33} = \dfrac{}{11}$ 10. $\dfrac{2}{3} = \dfrac{}{21}$ 14. $\dfrac{2}{9} = \dfrac{}{45}$

3. $\dfrac{4}{5} = \dfrac{}{20}$ 7. $\dfrac{4}{9} = \dfrac{}{27}$ 11. $\dfrac{20}{35} = \dfrac{}{7}$ 15. $\dfrac{6}{7} = \dfrac{}{49}$

4. $\dfrac{14}{16} = \dfrac{}{8}$ 8. $\dfrac{3}{5} = \dfrac{}{30}$ 12. $\dfrac{8}{9} = \dfrac{}{81}$ 16. $\dfrac{40}{64} = \dfrac{}{8}$

Find the least common denominator for each group of fractions below. Make sure you write the least common denominator every place where it should be.

17. $\dfrac{1}{3} = $ _____   19. $\dfrac{3}{8} = $ _____   21. $\dfrac{3}{7} = $ _____   23. Is it 12, 16, 24, or 48?

$\dfrac{3}{4} = $ _____ $\dfrac{1}{4} = $ _____ $\dfrac{1}{2} = $ _____ $\dfrac{3}{8} = $ _____

$\dfrac{2}{3} = $ _____

$\dfrac{5}{6} = $ _____

18. Is it 10, 30, 36, or 60?   20. $\dfrac{4}{9} = $ _____   22. $\dfrac{1}{2} = $ _____   24. $\dfrac{1}{3} = $ _____

$\dfrac{2}{3} = $ _____ $\dfrac{1}{6} = $ _____ $\dfrac{3}{10} = $ _____ $\dfrac{3}{4} = $ _____

$\dfrac{5}{6} = $ _____ $\dfrac{2}{3} = $ _____ $\dfrac{4}{5} = $ _____ $\dfrac{5}{8} = $ _____

$\dfrac{4}{5} = $ _____

Find the equivalent fractions in the problems below.

1. $\dfrac{2}{3} = \dfrac{}{6}$ 3. $\dfrac{4}{5} = \dfrac{}{25}$ 5. $\dfrac{3}{11} = \dfrac{}{22}$ 7. $\dfrac{5}{6} = \dfrac{}{42}$ 9. $\dfrac{4}{9} = \dfrac{}{45}$

2. $\dfrac{1}{2} = \dfrac{}{24}$ 4. $\dfrac{5}{8} = \dfrac{}{24}$ 6. $\dfrac{5}{5} = \dfrac{}{20}$ 8. $\dfrac{3}{7} = \dfrac{}{28}$ 10. $\dfrac{5}{6} = \dfrac{}{18}$

Now find the least common denominator for each group of fractions below. Make sure you write the least common denominator every place where it should be.

11. Is it 20, 10, or 40?

$\dfrac{1}{5} = \rule{2cm}{0.4pt}$

$\dfrac{1}{2} = \rule{2cm}{0.4pt}$

$\dfrac{3}{4} = \rule{2cm}{0.4pt}$

12. Is it 14, 28, or 42?

$\dfrac{4}{7} = \rule{2cm}{0.4pt}$

$\dfrac{1}{4} = \rule{2cm}{0.4pt}$

$\dfrac{1}{2} = \rule{2cm}{0.4pt}$

13. $\dfrac{5}{6} = \rule{2cm}{0.4pt}$

$\dfrac{1}{3} = \rule{2cm}{0.4pt}$

$\dfrac{3}{4} = \rule{2cm}{0.4pt}$

$\dfrac{1}{2} = \rule{2cm}{0.4pt}$

1. Find the interval, and figure out what *A* is on the following number line.

25   A   45

A = _____

2. Write 600,000 in words.

_____

Write four hundred twenty-nine trillion in numbers.

_____

3. Factor 26. _____

4. 72575 ÷ 9 = _____

5. Find the average of 16, 23, 19, 11, and 21.

_____

6. Write 7.003 in words.

_____

Write four and one tenth in decimals.

_____

7. 291.5 + 7 + 8.471 = _____

8. 91.5 − 26.258 = _____

9. Round off 89,623,210 to the nearest million.

_____

10. Round off .4735897 to the nearest hundredth.

_____

11. 8.47 × 26 = _____

12. Write MDCCCLXIX as an Arabic number.

_____

Write 3,334 in Roman numerals.

_____

13. 12.816 ÷ .48 = _____

14. Seven squared = _____

$9^2 =$ _____

15. What fraction of the circle is shaded in?

_____

16. If $\dfrac{11}{21}$ of a class is boys, what fraction is girls?

_____

To find *ratios* divide the first number into the second number and multiply the answer by the third number.

Example:

4 is to 12 as 5 is to **15** or $\dfrac{4}{12} = \dfrac{5}{15}$ ← This line means " is to."

$4\overline{)12}^{\,3}$ $3 \times 5 = $ **15**

Do the following ratio problems.

1. 9 is to 18 as 3 is to _____ or $\dfrac{9}{18} = \dfrac{3}{\rule{1cm}{0.4pt}}$

2. 2 is to 8 as 3 is to _____ or $\dfrac{2}{8} = \dfrac{\rule{0.7cm}{0.4pt}}{\rule{0.7cm}{0.4pt}}$

3. 5 is to 15 as 6 is to _____ or $\dfrac{5}{15} = \dfrac{\rule{0.7cm}{0.4pt}}{\rule{0.7cm}{0.4pt}}$

4. 10 is to 20 as 11 is to _____ or $\dfrac{10}{\rule{0.7cm}{0.4pt}} = \dfrac{\rule{0.7cm}{0.4pt}}{\rule{0.7cm}{0.4pt}}$

5. 7 is to 14 as 8 is to _____ or $\dfrac{7}{\rule{0.7cm}{0.4pt}} = \dfrac{\rule{0.7cm}{0.4pt}}{\rule{0.7cm}{0.4pt}}$

6. 8 is to 24 as 6 is to _____ or $\dfrac{\rule{0.7cm}{0.4pt}}{\rule{0.7cm}{0.4pt}} = \dfrac{\rule{0.7cm}{0.4pt}}{\rule{0.7cm}{0.4pt}}$

7. 3 is to 15 as 4 is to _____ or $\dfrac{\rule{0.7cm}{0.4pt}}{\rule{0.7cm}{0.4pt}} = \dfrac{\rule{0.7cm}{0.4pt}}{\rule{0.7cm}{0.4pt}}$

8. 7 is to 21 as 10 is to _____ or $\dfrac{\rule{0.7cm}{0.4pt}}{\rule{0.7cm}{0.4pt}} = \dfrac{\rule{0.7cm}{0.4pt}}{\rule{0.7cm}{0.4pt}}$

9. 2 is to 6 as 4 is to _____ or $\dfrac{\rule{0.7cm}{0.4pt}}{\rule{0.7cm}{0.4pt}} = \dfrac{\rule{0.7cm}{0.4pt}}{\rule{0.7cm}{0.4pt}}$

10. 10 is to 50 as 6 is to _____ or $\dfrac{\rule{0.7cm}{0.4pt}}{\rule{0.7cm}{0.4pt}} = \dfrac{\rule{0.7cm}{0.4pt}}{\rule{0.7cm}{0.4pt}}$

11. 8 is to 56 as 9 is to _____ or $\dfrac{\rule{0.7cm}{0.4pt}}{\rule{0.7cm}{0.4pt}} = \dfrac{\rule{0.7cm}{0.4pt}}{\rule{0.7cm}{0.4pt}}$

12. 2 is to 10 as 4 is to _____ or $\dfrac{\rule{0.7cm}{0.4pt}}{\rule{0.7cm}{0.4pt}} = \dfrac{\rule{0.7cm}{0.4pt}}{\rule{0.7cm}{0.4pt}}$

13. 7 is to 56 as 8 is to _____ or $\dfrac{\rule{0.7cm}{0.4pt}}{\rule{0.7cm}{0.4pt}} = \dfrac{\rule{0.7cm}{0.4pt}}{\rule{0.7cm}{0.4pt}}$

14. 6 is to 24 as 7 is to _____ or $\dfrac{\rule{0.7cm}{0.4pt}}{\rule{0.7cm}{0.4pt}} = \dfrac{\rule{0.7cm}{0.4pt}}{\rule{0.7cm}{0.4pt}}$

Use the same method as you used above to work out the next three problems.

15. 2 pieces of candy cost 12 cents, so 5 pieces of candy would cost _____ cents.

16. 3 postcards cost 60 cents, so 4 postcards would cost _____ cents.

17. 5 pencils cost 95 cents, so 3 pencils would cost _____ cents.

Work out the following ratio problems.

Remember: Divide the first number into the second, and then multiply the answer by the third number.

1. 7 is to 35 as 8 is to _____ or $\frac{7}{35} = \frac{8}{}$

2. 6 is to 54 as 7 is to _____ or $\frac{6}{54} = \underline{}$

3. 5 is to 25 as 4 is to _____ or $\frac{5}{} = \underline{}$

4. 12 is to 36 as 5 is to _____ or $\frac{}{} = \underline{}$

5. 6 is to 30 as 7 is to _____ or $\frac{}{} = \underline{}$

6. 2 is to 12 as 3 is to _____ or $\frac{}{} = \underline{}$

7. 8 is to 24 as 9 is to _____ or $\frac{}{} = \underline{}$

8. 4 is to 36 as 6 is to _____ or $\frac{}{} = \underline{}$

9. 6 is to 18 as 9 is to _____ or $\frac{}{} = \underline{}$

10. 7 is to 28 as 8 is to _____ or $\frac{}{} = \underline{}$

11. 12 is to 24 as 11 is to _____ or $\frac{}{} = \underline{}$

Note that the colon (:) is short for "is to."

12. 6 : 36 = 7 : _____

13. 9 : 63 = 10 : _____

14. 3 : 30 = 5 : _____

15. 8 : 32 = 9 : _____

16. 4 : 16 = 6 : _____

17. 9 : 18 = 8 : _____

Use the same method as you used above to work out the next two problems.

18. 2 tires cost $50, so 5 tires would cost _____.

19. 6 cans of juice cost $3.00, so 7 cans would cost _____.

Find equivalent fractions by putting the correct numerator over each denominator.

1. $\dfrac{4}{5} = \dfrac{}{15}$ 5. $\dfrac{12}{24} = \dfrac{}{48}$

2. $\dfrac{1}{8} = \dfrac{}{16}$ 6. $\dfrac{1}{2} = \dfrac{}{100}$

3. $\dfrac{5}{7} = \dfrac{}{35}$ 7. $\dfrac{9}{11} = \dfrac{}{44}$

4. $\dfrac{9}{10} = \dfrac{}{30}$

Do the following problems.

8. $\dfrac{9}{13} - \dfrac{3}{13} =$ 10. $\dfrac{3}{19} + \dfrac{14}{19} =$

9. $\dfrac{4}{7} + \dfrac{2}{7} =$

11. If $\dfrac{8}{11}$ of a pie is eaten, how much is left?

12. If $\dfrac{57}{100}$ a ship is underwater, what fraction is above water?

13. Write fourteen million in numbers.

14. Factors of 80 = _____ _____

_____ _____

15. $25264 \div 9 =$ _____

16. $8^2 =$ _____

17. Find the average of 99, 13, and 53.

18. Write MMCMLXIV in Arabic numbers.

19. Write 14.01 in words.

20. Write two and eighteen thousandths in decimals.

21. $2.89 + 40 + 1.3 =$ _____

22. $45 - 2.371 =$ _____

23. Round off .77731 to the nearest hundredth.

24. Round off 88.5931 to the nearest one.

25. $78.4 \times .52 =$ _____

26. $4555.2 \div 73 =$ _____

27. Five squared + nine squared + three cubed =

28. How many days are in February in a non-leap year?

29. Circle the measures of distance.
kilograms
inches
pounds
liters
centimeters
kilometers
milligrams
miles
meters
ounces

30. A cross-country runner ran 24.3 miles in 2.7 hours. How fast was she running in miles per hour?

31. Beverly weighs 119 pounds on Earth, but she would weigh .38 of that on Mars. What would she weigh on Mars?

_____

32. How many pounds are in a ton? _____

33. How many ounces are in a pound? _____

34. How many cups are in a pint? _____

35. How many quarts are in a gallon? _____

36. How many cents are in a half dollar? _____

37. How many hours are in a day? _____

Ratios 3

Work out the following ratio problems.

1. 6 : 12 = 7 : _____
2. 4 : 28 = 8 : _____
3. 2 : 20 = 9 : _____
4. 2 : 14 = 3 : _____
5. 5 : 60 = 6 : _____
6. 4 : 16 = 7 : _____
7. 7 : 14 = 9 : _____
8. 5 : 55 = 6 : _____
9. 12 : 60 = 11 : _____
10. 6 : 42 = 9 : _____
11. 4 : 36 = 8 : _____
12. 9 : 90 = 5 : _____
13. 6 : 36 = 5 : _____
14. 3 : 21 = 12 : _____
15. 9 : 36 = 4 : _____

16. 5 : 25 = 7 : _____
17. 7 : 56 = 9 : _____
18. 2 : 22 = 5 : _____
19. 10 : 100 = 9 : _____
20. 4 : 48 = 6 : _____
21. 3 : 60 = 5 : _____
22. 11 : 22 = 12 : _____
23. 9 : 81 = 7 : _____
24. 5 : 20 = 6 : _____
25. 3 : 30 = 5 : _____
26. 2 : 18 = 8 : _____
27. 3 : 33 = 4 : _____
28. 5 : 35 = 4 : _____
29. 6 : 42 = 2 : _____
30. 7 : 28 = 8 : _____

Now use the same method as you used above to work out the following word problems.

31. 3 small bags of popcorn cost 90 cents, so 2 bags will cost _____.

32. 6 pieces of candy cost 66 cents, so 8 pieces will cost _____.

33. 2 pencils cost 60 cents, so 4 pencils will cost _____.

34. 3 pens cost 72 cents, so 4 will cost _____.

Carefully work out the following ratio problems.

1. 6 : 24 = 7 : _____

2. 3 : 36 = 8 : _____

3. 5 : 40 = 9 : _____

4. 2 : 12 = 4 : _____

5. 4 : 28 = 9 : _____

6. 3 : 33 = 7 : _____

7. 12 : 48 = 5 : _____

8. 9 : 27 = 4 : _____

9. 6 : 54 = 5 : _____

10. 2 : 22 = 7 : _____

11. 4 : 48 = 5 : _____

12. 6 : 60 = 4 : _____

13. 13 : 26 = 3 : _____

14. 7 : 49 = 5 : _____

Here are some more ratio problems. These are a little tricky, so be careful.

15. 5 : 25 = _____ : 30

16. 4 : 12 = _____ : 9

17. 3 : 30 = _____ : 50

18. 6 : 36 = _____ : 48

19. 4 : 16 = _____ : 20

20. 7 : 21 = _____ : 27

21. 3 : 21 = _____ : 49

22. 4 : 44 = _____ : 55

23. 6 : 12 = _____ : 24

24. 9 : 36 = _____ : 44

25. 6 : 24 = _____ : 20

26. 4 : 28 = _____ : 35

Now work out the following word problems.

27. 2 games cost 6 dollars; how much would 3 games cost? _____.

28. 3 apples cost 75 cents, so 5 would cost _____.

29. 4 bags of marbles cost 3 dollars, so 2 bags would cost _____.

30. 5 erasers cost 45 cents, so 10 would cost _____.

Test 22 — Ratios

Work out the following ratio problems.

1. 2 is to 14 as 3 is to _____

2. 6 is to 12 as 8 is to _____

3. 5 : 25 = 7 : _____

4. 9 : 27 = 7 : _____

5. 10 : 30 = 3 : _____

6. 4 : 16 = 5 : _____

7. 12 : 36 = 2 : _____

8. 7 : 63 = 5 : _____

9. 4 : 48 = 5 : _____

10. 4 : 40 = 2 : _____

11. 5 : 55 = 2 : _____

12. 7 : 49 = 6 : _____

13. 9 : 90 = 3 : _____

14. 5 : 45 = 7 : _____

15. 8 : 32 = 5 : _____

16. 9 : 45 = 6 : _____

17. 6 : 18 = _____ : 21

18. 5 : 35 = _____ : 63

19. If 3 pieces of candy cost 24 cents, 5 will cost _____.

20. If 5 cans of juice cost $6.00, 3 cans will cost _____.

1. Find the interval, and figure out what *A* is on the following number line.

   23   A   27

   A = _____

2. Write 702,000,000,000,000 in words.

   _____

   Write ninety-seven billion in numbers.

   _____

3. Factor 27. _____

4. $63727 \div 7 =$ _____

5. Find the average of 628 and 500.

   _____

6. Write 9.013 in words.

   _____

   Write two and one hundredths in decimals.

   _____

7. $69 + 4.2 + 115.37 =$ _____

8. $26.4 - 18.268 =$ _____

9. Round off 268,721 to the nearest thousand.

   _____

10. Round off .3547219 to the nearest hundredth.

    _____

11. $2.47 \times .37 =$ _____

12. Write MMMXIII as an Arabic number.

    _____

    Write 2,747 in Roman numerals.

    _____

13. $684.32 \div 9.1 =$ _____

14. Two cubed = _____

    $3^5 =$ _____

15. What fraction of the circle is shaded in?

     _____

16. If $\dfrac{2}{19}$ of a test is wrong, what fraction is right?

    _____

To add or subtract fractions, the denominators must be the same. If they are not the same to start with, you have to change them to the least common denominator.

Least common denominators have been found for the following groups of fractions. First, find new numerators to put over the least common denominators. (Notice that you are finding equivalent fractions.) Then, add or subtract the numerators (tops).

Example:

$$\frac{2}{3} = \frac{8}{12}$$

$$+\frac{1}{4} = \frac{3}{12}$$

Answer $= \dfrac{11}{12}$

1. $\dfrac{5}{9} = \dfrac{}{9}$

$+\dfrac{1}{3} = \dfrac{}{9}$

2. $\dfrac{2}{9} = \dfrac{}{36}$

$+\dfrac{3}{4} = \dfrac{}{36}$

3. $\dfrac{2}{5} = \dfrac{}{15}$

$+\dfrac{1}{3} = \dfrac{}{15}$

4. $\dfrac{2}{3} = \dfrac{}{6}$

$-\dfrac{1}{6} = \dfrac{}{6}$

5. $\dfrac{8}{9} = \dfrac{}{18}$

$-\dfrac{5}{6} = \dfrac{}{18}$

6. $\dfrac{7}{8} = \dfrac{}{24}$

$-\dfrac{2}{3} = \dfrac{}{24}$

7. $\dfrac{4}{9} = \dfrac{}{18}$

$+\dfrac{1}{2} = \dfrac{}{18}$

8. $\dfrac{1}{11} = \dfrac{}{22}$

$+\dfrac{1}{2} = \dfrac{}{22}$

Find new numerators to put over the least common denominators. Then add or subtract the numerators.

1.
$$\frac{4}{5} = \frac{}{30}$$
$$+ \frac{1}{6} = \frac{}{30}$$
$$\overline{\qquad \frac{}{30}}$$

3.
$$\frac{3}{4} = \frac{}{12}$$
$$- \frac{2}{3} = \frac{}{12}$$
$$\overline{\qquad}$$

5.
$$\frac{5}{9} = \frac{}{9}$$
$$+ \frac{1}{3} = \frac{}{9}$$
$$\overline{\qquad}$$

7.
$$\frac{2}{3} = \frac{}{24}$$
$$- \frac{1}{8} = \frac{}{24}$$
$$\overline{\qquad}$$

2.
$$\frac{6}{7} = \frac{}{14}$$
$$- \frac{1}{2} = \frac{}{14}$$
$$\overline{\qquad}$$

4.
$$\frac{7}{8} = \frac{}{40}$$
$$- \frac{3}{5} = \frac{}{40}$$
$$\overline{\qquad}$$

6.
$$\frac{2}{7} = \frac{}{21}$$
$$+ \frac{2}{3} = \frac{}{21}$$
$$\overline{\qquad}$$

8.
$$\frac{5}{8} = \frac{}{8}$$
$$- \frac{1}{4} = \frac{}{8}$$
$$\overline{\qquad}$$

In the following problems, find the least common denominator. (Look for the smallest number that both the denominators will divide into evenly.) Then work out the problems by following the same steps as you used for the problems above.

9. Is the common denominator 4, 6, or 8?
$$\frac{1}{3} = \frac{}{\qquad}$$
$$+ \frac{1}{2} = \frac{}{\qquad}$$
$$\overline{\qquad}$$

10. Is the common denominator 8, 10, or 12?
$$\frac{2}{3} = \frac{}{\qquad}$$
$$+ \frac{1}{4} = \frac{}{\qquad}$$
$$\overline{\qquad}$$

11.
$$\frac{3}{8} = \frac{}{\qquad}$$
$$- \frac{1}{3} = \frac{}{\qquad}$$
$$\overline{\qquad}$$

12.
$$\frac{6}{7} = \frac{}{\qquad}$$
$$- \frac{2}{3} = \frac{}{\qquad}$$
$$\overline{\qquad}$$

13.
$$\frac{2}{5} = \frac{}{\qquad}$$
$$+ \frac{1}{4} = \frac{}{\qquad}$$
$$\overline{\qquad}$$

14.
$$\frac{1}{9} = \frac{}{\qquad}$$
$$+ \frac{2}{3} = \frac{}{\qquad}$$
$$\overline{\qquad}$$

15.
$$\frac{5}{6} = \frac{}{\qquad}$$
$$- \frac{1}{3} = \frac{}{\qquad}$$
$$\overline{\qquad}$$

16.
$$\frac{2}{7} = \frac{}{\qquad}$$
$$+ \frac{1}{4} = \frac{}{\qquad}$$
$$\overline{\qquad}$$

1. Figure out what *A* is on the following number line.

   23   A   28

   A = _____

2. Write 19,000,000,000,000 in words.

   _____

3. Factors of 56 = _____ _____

   _____

4. 42238 ÷ 7 = _____

5. 4 : 44 = _____ : 66

6. 9 : 45 = 4 : _____

7. 10 : 20 = 100 : _____

8. 12 : 36 = _____ : 9

9. Find the average of 713 and 515.

   _____

10. Write ten and seventeen thousandths in decimals.

    _____

11. 74 − 21.428 = _____

12. 2.4 + 35 + .17 = _____

13. Round off .44568 to the nearest thousandth.

    _____

14. Round off 78.472 to the nearest one.

    _____

15. 8.21 × 3.7 = _____

16. 6.822 ÷ 1.8 = _____

17. Circle the measures of weight.

    miles
    kilograms
    pounds
    centimeters
    inches
    ounces
    kilometers
    tons
    grams

18. How many days are in July? _____

19. How many days are in September? _____

20. $7^2 + 5^3 =$ _____

21. Three to the sixth = _____

22. How far along the inch is *A*? Use a fraction to answer.

    A

    A = _____

23. Write MMCLXVIII as an Arabic number.

    _____

24. Write 3,234 in Roman numerals.

    _____

25. Howard and La Keisha did $\frac{3}{4}$ of a job. How much remained to be done?

    _____

    Rosa read 28 pages an hour as she made her way through a detective novel. It took her exactly 6.5 hours to read the book. How many pages did the book have?

    _____

27. How many cents are in a quarter? _____

28. How many cents are in five nickels? _____

29. How many cents are in nine dimes? _____

30. How many days are in seventeen weeks? _____

31. How many ounces are in a pound? _____

32. How many pounds are in a ton? _____

33. How many cups are in a pint? _____

34. How many pints are in a quart? _____

35. How many quarts are in a gallon? _____

36. How many inches are in a foot? _____

37. How many feet are in a mile? _____

38. How many seconds are in a minute? _____

To solve the problems below, use the following steps:
1) Find the least common denominator.
2) Find the numerators (tops) to put over the least common denominators.
3) Add or subtract the numerators.

1. $\dfrac{3}{5} =$ ———

$+ \dfrac{1}{4} =$ ———

———

2. $\dfrac{3}{8} =$ ———

$+ \dfrac{1}{6} =$ ———

3. $\dfrac{4}{9} =$

$+ \dfrac{1}{3} =$

4. $\dfrac{2}{3} =$

$+ \dfrac{1}{7} =$

5. $\dfrac{8}{9} =$

$- \dfrac{5}{6} =$

6. $\dfrac{5}{6} =$

$+ \dfrac{1}{4} =$

7. $\dfrac{4}{5} =$

$- \dfrac{2}{3} =$

8. $\dfrac{1}{3} =$

$+ \dfrac{3}{10} =$

9. $\dfrac{6}{7} =$

$- \dfrac{1}{2} =$

10. $\dfrac{3}{8} =$

$+ \dfrac{1}{3} =$

11. $\dfrac{4}{9} =$

$+ \dfrac{1}{4} =$

12. $\dfrac{5}{8} =$

$+ \dfrac{1}{5} =$

Each of the following problems contains three fractions. To solve these problems, use the same steps as you used for the problems above.

13. $\dfrac{1}{3} =$ ———

$\dfrac{1}{4} =$ ———

$+ \dfrac{1}{2} =$ ———

14. $\dfrac{1}{2} =$ ———

$\dfrac{1}{6} =$ ———

$+ \dfrac{1}{4} =$ ———

15. $\dfrac{1}{10} =$ ———

$\dfrac{1}{3} =$ ———

$+ \dfrac{1}{5} =$

To solve the problems below, use the following steps:

1) Find the least common denominator.
2) Find the numerators (tops) to put over the least common denominators.
3) Add or subtract the numerators.

1. $\dfrac{1}{6} = $ ——
   $+\dfrac{3}{5} = $ ——
   ——

5. $\dfrac{3}{4}$
   $-\dfrac{1}{3}$

9. $\dfrac{8}{9}$
   $-\dfrac{1}{2}$

13. $\dfrac{4}{5}$
    $+\dfrac{1}{7}$

2. $\dfrac{7}{8}$
   $-\dfrac{1}{3}$

6. $\dfrac{4}{11}$
   $+\dfrac{1}{2}$

10. $\dfrac{2}{5}$
    $+\dfrac{1}{4}$

14. $\dfrac{1}{2}$
    $+\dfrac{3}{8}$

3. $\dfrac{5}{6}$
   $-\dfrac{3}{8}$

7. $\dfrac{2}{7}$
   $+\dfrac{1}{4}$

11. $\dfrac{9}{10}$
    $-\dfrac{2}{3}$

15. $\dfrac{5}{6}$
    $-\dfrac{4}{9}$

4. $\dfrac{1}{2}$
   $\dfrac{1}{3}$
   $+\dfrac{1}{8}$

8. $\dfrac{1}{3}$
   $\dfrac{1}{4}$
   $+\dfrac{1}{6}$

12. $\dfrac{1}{5}$
    $\dfrac{1}{6}$
    $+\dfrac{3}{10}$

16. $\dfrac{1}{3}$
    $\dfrac{1}{9}$
    $+\dfrac{1}{6}$

Arrange the fractions in the following problems one above the other. Then work out each problem and put the answers on this page.

17. $\dfrac{1}{7} + \dfrac{2}{3} = $ _____

18. $\dfrac{4}{5} - \dfrac{3}{7} = $ _____

19. $\dfrac{1}{10} + \dfrac{1}{2} = $ _____

Solve the following problems.

1. $\dfrac{3}{8}$

   $+\dfrac{1}{3}$
   _____

3. $\dfrac{3}{4}$

   $-\dfrac{1}{5}$
   _____

5. $\dfrac{5}{9}$

   $+\dfrac{1}{3}$
   _____

2. $\dfrac{1}{4}$

   $+\dfrac{1}{6}$
   _____

4. $\dfrac{7}{8}$

   $-\dfrac{5}{6}$
   _____

Now do the following problems. Remember to arrange the fractions one above the other before you work each one out.

6. $\dfrac{6}{7} - \dfrac{2}{3} =$ _____

8. $\dfrac{1}{6} + \dfrac{2}{9} =$ _____

10. $\dfrac{1}{5} + \dfrac{1}{6} + \dfrac{1}{3} =$ _____

7. $\dfrac{4}{7} + \dfrac{1}{5} =$ _____

9. $\dfrac{2}{3} - \dfrac{3}{10} =$ _____

1. Figure out what *A* is on the following number line.

   18   A   42

   A = _____

2. Write 230,000,000 in words.

   _____

   Write fourteen billion in numbers.

   _____

3. Factor 36 four ways. _____ _____

   _____ _____

4. 51225 ÷ 8 = _____

5. Find the average of 17, 23, and 32.

   _____

6. Write 7.18 in words.

   _____

   Write two and one thousandth in decimals.

   _____

7. 98 + 3.69 + 2.735 = _____

8. 16.8 − 4.231 = _____

9. Round off 69,575,214 to the nearest million.

   _____

10. Round off .443798 to the nearest tenth.

    _____

11. 685 × 3.7 = _____

12. Write MCDLXXXVIII as an Arabic number.

    _____

    Write 2,845 in Roman numerals.

    _____

13. 468.72 ÷ 6.2 = _____

14. Five cubed = _____

    4^2 = _____

15. What fraction of the circle is shaded in?

     _____

16. If $\frac{3}{7}$ of a job is finished, how much still has to be done?

    _____

17. Complete the ratio.

    6 : 18 = 8 : _____

Reducing fractions to their lowest terms is a way of making them easier to understand. To reduce a fraction, find the largest number that will divide evenly into the top and bottom. This number is called the *greatest common factor.* Divide it into the top and bottom, and then write the answers as the reduced fraction.

Example:

$$\frac{6}{12} = \underline{\hspace{2cm}}$$ The greatest common factor of 6 and 12 is 6.

$$\frac{6 \div 6}{12 \div 6} = \frac{1}{2}$$

Reduce the following fractions to their lowest terms. Before you begin each problem, write the greatest common factor in the circle.

1. (2)   is the greatest common factor.

   $$\frac{2 \div 2}{4 \div 2} = \underline{\hspace{2cm}}$$

2. (5)   is the greatest common factor.

   $$\frac{10 \div 5}{15 \div 5} = \underline{\hspace{2cm}}$$

3. (2) $\frac{6}{8} = \underline{\hspace{2cm}}$

4. (5) $\frac{5}{15} = \underline{\hspace{2cm}}$

5. ( ) $\frac{2}{8} = \underline{\hspace{2cm}}$

6. ( ) $\frac{12}{14} = \underline{\hspace{2cm}}$

7. ( ) $\frac{6}{12} = \underline{\hspace{2cm}}$

8. ( ) $\frac{4}{12} = \underline{\hspace{2cm}}$

9. ( ) $\frac{2}{16} = \underline{\hspace{2cm}}$

10. ( ) $\frac{8}{12} = \underline{\hspace{2cm}}$

11. ( ) $\frac{4}{6} = \underline{\hspace{2cm}}$

12. ( ) $\frac{2}{20} = \underline{\hspace{2cm}}$

13. ( ) $\frac{6}{8} = \underline{\hspace{2cm}}$

14. ( ) $\frac{18}{24} = \underline{\hspace{2cm}}$

15. ( ) $\frac{3}{15} = \underline{\hspace{2cm}}$

16. ( ) $\frac{6}{15} = \underline{\hspace{2cm}}$

17. ( ) $\frac{6}{18} = \underline{\hspace{2cm}}$

18. ( ) $\frac{4}{24} = \underline{\hspace{2cm}}$

19. ( ) $\frac{16}{20} = \underline{\hspace{2cm}}$

20. ( ) $\frac{9}{18} = \underline{\hspace{2cm}}$

21. ( ) $\frac{20}{30} = \underline{\hspace{2cm}}$

Reducing Fractions 2

Reduce each fraction below to its lowest terms. To do this, write the greatest common factor in the circle; then divide the greatest common factor into the top and bottom of the fraction.

1. (2) $\frac{6}{8}$ = _____

2. (4) $\frac{4}{8}$ = _____

3. (7) $\frac{7}{14}$ = _____

4. ◯ $\frac{3}{9}$ = _____

5. ◯ $\frac{5}{20}$ = _____

6. ◯ $\frac{12}{16}$ = _____

7. ◯ $\frac{7}{21}$ = _____

8. ◯ $\frac{14}{21}$ = _____

9. ◯ $\frac{4}{12}$ = _____

10. ◯ $\frac{5}{30}$ = _____

11. ◯ $\frac{6}{24}$ = _____

12. ◯ $\frac{6}{9}$ = _____

13. ◯ $\frac{10}{15}$ = _____

14. ◯ $\frac{8}{16}$ = _____

15. ◯ $\frac{4}{28}$ = _____

16. ◯ $\frac{7}{35}$ = _____

17. ◯ $\frac{6}{30}$ = _____

18. ◯ $\frac{12}{30}$ = _____

19. ◯ $\frac{8}{20}$ = _____

20. ◯ $\frac{2}{12}$ = _____

21. ◯ $\frac{10}{30}$ = _____

22. ◯ $\frac{9}{15}$ = _____

23. ◯ $\frac{6}{36}$ = _____

24. ◯ $\frac{4}{14}$ = _____

25. ◯ $\frac{2}{30}$ = _____

26. ◯ $\frac{5}{40}$ = _____

27. ◯ $\frac{9}{21}$ = _____

Review 24

1. $\frac{1}{3} + \frac{3}{8} =$ _____

2. $\frac{9}{10} - \frac{1}{3} =$ _____

3. $\frac{4}{5} - \frac{3}{4} =$ _____

4. $\frac{3}{7} + \frac{1}{3} =$ _____

5. $\frac{4}{5} - \frac{2}{3} =$ _____

6. $\frac{4}{7} + \frac{1}{4} =$ _____

7. Figure out what *A* is on the following number line.

```
35                    A      63
|     |       |        |      |
```

   A = _____

8. Write 44,000,000,000 in words.

   _____

9. Factors of 55 = _____

10. 7 : 49 = 9 : _____

11. 5 : 25 = _____ : 35

12. 210.945 ÷ .35 = _____

13. 79.1 × .68 = _____

14. Find the average of 371 and 203.

   _____

15. Write six and one tenth in decimals.

   _____

16. Write 7.011 in words.

   _____

17. 79 + 1.9 + 3.77 = _____

18. 22 − 1.73 = _____

Round off the following to the nearest ten.

19. 77 _____   20. 91 _____

21. Round off .834793 to the nearest hundredth.

   _____

22. Write MMCCXLVII as an Arabic number.

   _____

23. $5^2 + 7^3 =$ _____

24. Two to the seventh = _____

25. Mr. Spock's Cadillac went 286 miles on a full tank of 22 gallons of gas. How many miles is this gas-guzzler getting to the gallon?

   _____

26. A theater charged $7.25 per ticket, and only 93 people came to see the movie. How much did the theater make for that showing?

   _____

27. How many nickels are in a dollar? _____

28. How many dimes are in a dollar? _____

29. How many quarters are in a dollar? _____

30. How many half-dollars are in a dollar? _____

31. How many days are in February in a leap year?

   _____

32. How many days are in March? _____

33. How many days are in November? _____

34. How many quarts are in 4 gallons? _____

35. How many ounces are in 6 pounds? _____

36. How many days are in 6 weeks? _____

37. Circle the metric measure you would use to measure the water in a pot.

    milliter

    liter

38. Circle which metric measure you would use to measure the thickness of your fingernail.

    millimeter

    centimeter

    meter

    kilometer

39. Which metric measure would you use to measure the distance between your eyes?

_____

Reduce the following fractions to their lowest terms. Be careful; some of them don't need to be reduced.

1. $\dfrac{4}{8}$ = _____

2. $\dfrac{6}{12}$ = _____

3. $\dfrac{2}{3}$ = _____
   3

4. $\dfrac{7}{14}$ = _____

5. $\dfrac{2}{12}$ = _____

6. $\dfrac{4}{16}$ = _____

7. $\dfrac{8}{9}$ = _____

8. $\dfrac{11}{22}$ = _____

9. $\dfrac{9}{27}$ = _____

10. $\dfrac{14}{21}$ = _____

11. $\dfrac{6}{18}$ = _____

12. $\dfrac{3}{24}$ = _____

13. $\dfrac{8}{16}$ = _____

14. $\dfrac{4}{30}$ = _____

15. $\dfrac{9}{21}$ = _____

16. $\dfrac{7}{42}$ = _____

17. $\dfrac{2}{21}$ = _____

18. $\dfrac{8}{80}$ = _____

19. $\dfrac{16}{24}$ = _____

20. $\dfrac{18}{27}$ = _____

In the following problems, add or subtract, and then reduce the answer to the lowest terms if necessary.

21. $\dfrac{7}{8} - \dfrac{3}{8}$ = _____

22. $\dfrac{4}{15} + \dfrac{4}{15}$ = _____

23. $\dfrac{3}{10} + \dfrac{3}{10}$ = _____

24. $\dfrac{9}{14} - \dfrac{5}{14}$ = _____

25. $\dfrac{5}{9} - \dfrac{2}{9}$ = _____

26. $1\dfrac{1}{6} + 1\dfrac{1}{6}$ = _____

27. A woman jogged $\dfrac{5}{8}$ of a mile one day and $\dfrac{1}{8}$ of a mile the next. How far did she go in all?

_____

Reduce the following fractions to their lowest terms. If a fraction can't be reduced, just copy it the way it is — it's already in its lowest terms.

1. $\dfrac{4}{12}$ = _____

2. $\dfrac{7}{21}$ = _____

3. $\dfrac{6}{9}$ = _____

4. $\dfrac{8}{12}$ = _____

5. $\dfrac{11}{12}$ = _____

6. $\dfrac{15}{20}$ = _____

7. $\dfrac{6}{18}$ = _____

8. $\dfrac{4}{5}$ = _____

9. $\dfrac{8}{10}$ = _____

10. $\dfrac{10}{40}$ = _____

11. $\dfrac{6}{36}$ = _____

12. $\dfrac{14}{28}$ = _____

13. $\dfrac{16}{17}$ = _____

14. $\dfrac{2}{32}$ = _____

15. $\dfrac{9}{36}$ = _____

16. $\dfrac{4}{48}$ = _____

17. $\dfrac{2}{5}$ = _____

18. $\dfrac{15}{30}$ = _____

19. $\dfrac{8}{48}$ = _____

20. $\dfrac{2}{100}$ = _____

Now work out the following problems. If the answer needs to be reduced to its lowest terms, do so. If not, just leave it as it is.

21. $\dfrac{3}{10} + \dfrac{2}{10}$ = _____ = _____

22. $\dfrac{8}{15} + \dfrac{2}{15}$ = _____ = _____

23. $\dfrac{6}{10} + \dfrac{3}{10}$ = _____

24. $\dfrac{13}{20} - \dfrac{3}{20}$ = _____

Solve the following word problem.

25. A man painted $\dfrac{4}{15}$ of his house one day and $\dfrac{8}{15}$ the next. What fraction of the house was painted?

_____

What fraction did he still have to do?

_____

Reduce the following fractions to their lowest terms. If some of them can't be reduced, just copy them as they are.

1. $\dfrac{5}{10}$ = _____

2. $\dfrac{6}{8}$ = _____

3. $\dfrac{4}{5}$ = _____

4. $\dfrac{8}{16}$ = _____

5. $\dfrac{10}{40}$ = _____

6. $\dfrac{3}{18}$ = _____

7. $\dfrac{5}{35}$ = _____

8. $\dfrac{10}{12}$ = _____

9. $\dfrac{6}{36}$ = _____

10. $\dfrac{8}{40}$ = _____

11. $\dfrac{9}{17}$ = _____

12. $\dfrac{2}{22}$ = _____

13. $\dfrac{16}{32}$ = _____

14. $\dfrac{40}{50}$ = _____

15. $\dfrac{2}{28}$ = _____

16. $\dfrac{25}{100}$ = _____

Now work out the following problems. Make sure you give the answers in their lowest terms.

17. $\dfrac{4}{9} + \dfrac{2}{9}$ =

18. $\dfrac{6}{14} + \dfrac{1}{14}$ =

19. $\dfrac{4}{25} + \dfrac{9}{25}$ =

20. $\dfrac{19}{20} - \dfrac{4}{20}$ =

1. Figure out what *A* is on the following number line.

   20   A   100

   A = _____

2. Write 601,000 in words.

   _____

   Write five hundred billion in numbers.

   _____

3. Factor 22. _____

4. $31555 \div 9 =$ _____

5. Find the average of 123, 318, and 213.

   _____

6. Write 12.012 in words.

   _____

   Write four and two hundredths in decimals.

   _____

7. $9.6 + 17 + 293.42 =$ _____

8. $63.4 - 29.147 =$ _____

9. Round off 62,741 to the nearest thousand.

   _____

10. Round off .6375926 to the nearest thousandth.

    _____

11. $7.21 \times .47 =$ _____

12. Write MMMDCCLXXI as an Arabic number.

    _____

    Write 2,924 in Roman numerals.

    _____

13. $44.296 \div .56 =$ _____

14. Three squared = _____

    $5^3 =$ _____

15. What fraction of the circle is shaded in?

     _____

16. If $\dfrac{17}{29}$ of a hotel is filled, what fraction is empty?

    _____

17. Complete the ratio.

    $5 : 55 =$ _____ $: 77$

18. $\dfrac{2}{3} + \dfrac{1}{4} =$ _____

An *improper fraction* is one like $\frac{8}{3}$ in which the top is bigger than the bottom. If you get an improper fraction in the answer to a problem, you must change it to a *mixed number* for it to be correct.

Example:

Improper fraction → Mixed number

$$\frac{8}{3} = 2\frac{2}{3}$$

Shade in the circles below. Look at the improper fractions to see how many parts to shade in. Write a whole number to show how many whole circles are filled in, and write a fraction to show what is left over.

Example:

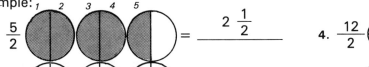

$\frac{5}{2}$ = $2\frac{1}{2}$ _____

1. $\frac{7}{3}$ = _____

2. $\frac{9}{4}$ = _____

3. $\frac{15}{8}$ = _____

4. $\frac{12}{2}$ = _____

5. $\frac{7}{6}$ = _____

6. $\frac{5}{4}$ = _____

7. $\frac{4}{2}$ = _____

There is an easier way to change improper fractions to mixed numbers. Follow these steps:

1) Divide the bottom of the fraction into the top.
2) Write the answer as a whole number.
3) Write the remainder (if there is one) as a numerator over the same denominator you started with.

Example:

$$\frac{7}{5} = \begin{array}{r} 1 \\ 5\overline{)7} \\ \underline{5} \\ 2 \end{array} = 1\frac{2}{5} \text{ Answer}$$

Change the following improper fractions to mixed numbers.

8. $\frac{8}{2}$ = _____

9. $\frac{3}{2}$ = _____

10. $\frac{10}{3}$ = _____

11. $\frac{7}{2}$ = _____

12. $\frac{14}{5}$ = _____

13. $\frac{14}{3}$ = _____

14. $\frac{13}{2}$ = _____

15. $\frac{13}{10}$ = _____

16. $\frac{5}{3}$ = _____

Change the following improper fractions to mixed numbers.
Remember the three steps to follow:
1) Divide the bottom of the fraction into the top.
2) Write the answer as a whole number.
3) Write the remainder (if any) as a numerator over the same denominator you started with.

Example:

$$\frac{7}{3} = 2\frac{1}{3}$$

1. $\frac{5}{4}$ = _____ 　 4. $\frac{10}{3}$ = _____ 　 7. $\frac{3}{3}$ = _____ 　 10. $\frac{9}{5}$ = _____ 　 13. $\frac{9}{9}$ = _____

2. $\frac{9}{2}$ = _____ 　 5. $\frac{12}{5}$ = _____ 　 8. $\frac{15}{7}$ = _____ 　 11. $\frac{17}{8}$ = _____ 　 14. $\frac{21}{10}$ = _____

3. $\frac{4}{2}$ = _____ 　 6. $\frac{8}{7}$ = _____ 　 9. $\frac{5}{4}$ = _____ 　 12. $\frac{14}{7}$ = _____ 　 15. $\frac{17}{2}$ = _____

To change mixed numbers back into improper fractions, use the following steps:
1) Multiply the bottom of the fraction by the whole number.
2) Add the top of the fraction to the answer.
3) Write that answer as the top of a fraction with the same denominator that you started with on the bottom.

Example:

$$2\frac{3}{4} = \frac{11}{4} \ (4 \times 2 = 8 + 3 = 11)$$

Change the following mixed numbers to improper fractions.

16. $2\frac{2}{3}$ = $\frac{}{3}$ 　 19. $1\frac{1}{4}$ = _____ 　 22. $6\frac{1}{8}$ = _____ 　 25. $10\frac{1}{3}$ = _____

17. $4\frac{1}{3}$ = _____ 　 20. $2\frac{5}{9}$ = _____ 　 23. $1\frac{9}{10}$ = _____ 　 26. $4\frac{6}{7}$ = _____

18. $5\frac{2}{3}$ = _____ 　 21. $4\frac{3}{8}$ = _____ 　 24. $5\frac{7}{8}$ = _____ 　 27. $7\frac{1}{2}$ = _____

Reduce the following fractions to lowest terms.

1. $\dfrac{4}{6}$ = _____

2. $\dfrac{9}{21}$ = _____

3. $\dfrac{4}{6}$ = _____

4. $\dfrac{6}{9}$ = _____

5. $\dfrac{7}{49}$ = _____

6. $\dfrac{4}{20}$ = _____

7. $\dfrac{5}{25}$ = _____

8. $\dfrac{21}{24}$ = _____

9. $\dfrac{30}{33}$ = _____

10. $\dfrac{3}{15}$ = _____

11. $\dfrac{9}{15}$ = _____

12. Figure out what *A* is on the following number line.

```
12                    A      40
 |  |  |  |  |  |  |  |  |
```

   A = _____

13. 7 : 14 = 8 : _____   14. 3 : 12 = _____ : 20

15. 5581 × .23 = _____

16. 460.734 ÷ .51 = _____

17. Round off 29512 to the nearest thousand.

   _____

18. Round off 6.9343789 to the nearest thousandth.

   _____

19. Write MMCCLXXXII in Arabic numbers.

   _____

20. Write 3,428 in Roman numerals.

   _____

21. $\dfrac{9}{10}$ + $\dfrac{1}{3}$ = _____

22. $\dfrac{6}{7}$ − $\dfrac{1}{3}$ = _____

23. $\dfrac{3}{4}$ − $\dfrac{1}{8}$ = _____

24. $\dfrac{2}{5}$ + $\dfrac{1}{3}$ = _____

25. Find the average of 636, 213, and 420.

   _____

26. 7^3 = _____

27. Five to the fourth = _____

28. Factors of 81 = _____ _____

29. Write 6.05 in words.

   _____

30. Write nine hundred thirty-eight billion in numbers.

   _____

31. 47.8 + 9.731 = _____

32. 30 − 2.18 = _____

33. Circle the best metric measure to use to measure a basketball court.
   millimeters
   centimeters
   meters
   kilometers

34. Which metric measure would be best to measure this piece of paper?

   _____

35. Circle the best metric measure to use to measure the weight of a dog.
   milligrams
   grams
   kilograms

36. How many seconds are in a minute?

   _____

37. How many minutes are in an hour? _____

38. How many hours are in a day? _____

39. How many days are in a week? _____

40. How many days are in a year? _____

41. How many days are in a leap year? _____

42. How many inches are in a foot? _____

43. How many inches are in a yard? _____

44. How many feet are in a mile? _____

45. How many cups are in a pint? _____

46. A bicycle racer covered 595 miles going 35 miles an hour. How long did this take?

_____

47. A woman decided that she liked dimes. She went to the bank and asked for $189.90 worth of dimes. How many dimes did she get?

_____

Do you think they'd give that many dimes to her? Why?

_____

Change the following improper fractions to mixed numbers.

Example:

$$\frac{5}{3} = 1\frac{2}{3}$$

1. $\frac{8}{2} =$ _____

3. $\frac{7}{6} =$ _____

5. $\frac{15}{7} =$ _____

7. $\frac{23}{7} =$ _____

2. $\frac{10}{7} =$ _____

4. $\frac{12}{3} =$ _____

6. $\frac{9}{2} =$ _____

8. $\frac{14}{3} =$ _____

Change the following mixed numbers to improper fractions.

9. $2\frac{1}{3} = \frac{}{3}$

12. $9\frac{2}{5} =$ _____

15. $12\frac{1}{2} =$ _____

10. $4\frac{3}{4} =$ _____

13. $5\frac{1}{2} =$ _____

16. $6\frac{2}{9} =$ _____

11. $6\frac{1}{2} =$ _____

14. $7\frac{4}{7} =$ _____

17. $11\frac{3}{5} =$ _____

Now work out the answers to the following problems. If an answer is an improper fraction, change it to a mixed number.

18. $\frac{5}{8} + \frac{7}{8} = \frac{}{8} =$ _____

21. $\frac{7}{9} + \frac{8}{9} + \frac{3}{9} = \frac{}{} =$ _____

19. $\frac{2}{3} + \frac{2}{3} = \frac{}{} =$ _____

22. $\frac{4}{5} + \frac{3}{5} + \frac{4}{5} = \frac{}{} =$ _____

20. $\frac{4}{5} + \frac{3}{5} = \frac{}{} =$ _____

23. $\frac{7}{8} + \frac{6}{8} + \frac{5}{8} = \frac{}{} =$ _____

24. $\frac{3}{4} = \frac{}{}$

$+ \frac{4}{5} = \frac{}{}$

25. $\frac{7}{8} = \frac{}{}$

$+ \frac{4}{5} = \frac{}{}$

Improper Fractions and Mixed Numbers 4

Change the following improper fractions to mixed numbers.

1. $\dfrac{7}{2}$ = _____

2. $\dfrac{5}{3}$ = _____

3. $\dfrac{10}{2}$ = _____

4. $\dfrac{14}{3}$ = _____

5. $\dfrac{24}{5}$ = _____

6. $\dfrac{6}{5}$ = _____

7. $\dfrac{18}{6}$ = _____

8. $\dfrac{24}{7}$ = _____

9. $\dfrac{19}{10}$ = _____

Change the following mixed numbers to improper fractions.

10. $6\,\dfrac{1}{3}$ = _____

11. $4\,\dfrac{2}{5}$ = _____

12. $9\,\dfrac{1}{2}$ = _____

13. $10\,\dfrac{3}{5}$ = _____

14. $1\,\dfrac{1}{5}$ = _____

15. $5\,\dfrac{2}{7}$ = _____

16. $2\,\dfrac{8}{9}$ = _____

17. $7\,\dfrac{1}{7}$ = _____

18. $11\,\dfrac{1}{5}$ = _____

Work out the following problems. If an answer is an improper fraction, change it to a mixed number.

19. $\dfrac{1}{3} + \dfrac{2}{3} + \dfrac{2}{3} = \dfrac{}{} =$ _____

20. $\dfrac{3}{7} + \dfrac{4}{7} + \dfrac{6}{7} = \dfrac{}{} =$ _____

21. $\dfrac{2}{9} + \dfrac{8}{9} + \dfrac{5}{9} = \dfrac{}{} =$ _____

22. $\dfrac{4}{5} + \dfrac{4}{5} + \dfrac{4}{5} = \dfrac{}{} =$ _____

23. $\dfrac{9}{10} + \dfrac{7}{10} + \dfrac{5}{10} = \dfrac{}{} =$ _____

24. $\dfrac{14}{15} + \dfrac{13}{15} + \dfrac{8}{15} = \dfrac{}{} =$ _____

25. $\quad \dfrac{7}{8} = \dfrac{}{}$

$+ \quad \dfrac{4}{5} = \dfrac{}{}$

_____

Test 25 — Improper Fractions and Mixed Numbers

Change the following improper fractions to mixed numbers.

1. $\dfrac{5}{2}$ = _____

2. $\dfrac{17}{5}$ = _____

3. $\dfrac{4}{3}$ = _____

4. $\dfrac{25}{5}$ = _____

5. $\dfrac{7}{6}$ = _____

6. $\dfrac{10}{9}$ = _____

7. $\dfrac{28}{5}$ = _____

Change the following mixed numbers to improper fractions.

8. $4\dfrac{2}{3}$ = _____

9. $8\dfrac{1}{2}$ = _____

10. $3\dfrac{5}{6}$ = _____

11. $9\dfrac{2}{5}$ = _____

12. $16\dfrac{1}{2}$ = _____

13. $10\dfrac{5}{7}$ = _____

14. $9\dfrac{4}{5}$ = _____

Work out the following problems. Give the final answers as mixed numbers.

15. $\dfrac{4}{7} + \dfrac{5}{7} + \dfrac{6}{7}$ = —— = _____

16. $\dfrac{9}{10} + \dfrac{1}{10} + \dfrac{7}{10}$ = _____

17. $\dfrac{2}{3} + \dfrac{2}{3} + \dfrac{1}{3}$ = _____

18. $\dfrac{8}{9} + \dfrac{2}{9} + \dfrac{7}{9}$ = _____

19. $\quad \dfrac{4}{7}$ = ——

    $+ \quad \dfrac{2}{3}$ = ___

    _____

20. $\quad \dfrac{5}{9}$ = ___

    $+ \quad \dfrac{4}{5}$ = ___

    _____

1. Figure out what *A* is on the following number line.

   16   A   24

   A = _____

2. Write 219,000,000,000 in words.

   _____

   _____

   Write three hundred trillion in numbers.

   _____

3. Factor 28 two ways. _____ _____

4. 42379 ÷ 7 = _____

5. Find the average of 18 and 26.

   _____

6. Write 3.005 in words.

   _____

   Write thirteen and twelve hundredths in decimals.

   _____

7. 69 + 3.47 + 1.891 = _____

8. 26.5 − 18.268 = _____

9. Round off 485,621,313 to the nearest million.

   _____

10. Round off 29.37842 to the nearest one.

    _____

11. 9.03 × 48 = _____

12. Write MMCDLXVI as an Arabic number.

    _____

    Write 3,642 in Roman numerals.

    _____

13. 416.02 ÷ 6.2 = _____

14. Six squared = _____

    2^6 = _____

15. What fraction of the circle is shaded in?

     _____

16. If $\dfrac{13}{20}$ of a test is right, what fraction is wrong?

    _____

17. Complete the ratio.

    9 : 27 = 10 : _____

18. $\dfrac{6}{7} - \dfrac{1}{3}$ = _____

19. Reduce the following fractions to lowest terms.

    $\dfrac{8}{30}$ = _____ $\dfrac{5}{35}$ = _____

Work out the following problems. First add or subtract the fractions of each mixed number, then add or subtract the whole numbers.

Example:

$$2\frac{1}{3}$$
$$+4\frac{1}{3}$$
$$\overline{6\frac{2}{3}}$$

2. $$6\frac{1}{7}$$
$$+8\frac{4}{7}$$

4. $$10\frac{4}{11}$$
$$-2\frac{3}{11}$$

6. $$9\frac{4}{5}$$
$$-4\frac{1}{5}$$

1. $$9\frac{4}{9}$$
$$+7\frac{3}{9}$$

3. $$24\frac{3}{4}$$
$$-5\frac{2}{4}$$

5. $$10\frac{8}{9}$$
$$-5\frac{7}{9}$$

7. $$29\frac{3}{8}$$
$$+14\frac{4}{8}$$

Work out the following problems. If the fraction in the answer is an improper fraction, change it to a mixed number. Then add the whole number in the mixed number to the whole number you already have.

Example:

$$5\frac{2}{3}$$
$$+4\frac{2}{3}$$
$$\overline{9\frac{4}{3}} =$$
$$9 + 1\frac{1}{3} = 10\frac{1}{3}$$

9. $$7\frac{4}{5}$$
$$+8\frac{3}{5}$$

11. $$4\frac{6}{7}$$
$$+8\frac{3}{7}$$

8. $$4\frac{5}{8}$$
$$+7\frac{3}{8}$$

10. $$12\frac{4}{11}$$
$$+10\frac{2}{11}$$

12. $$12\frac{7}{9}$$
$$+5\frac{8}{9}$$

Extra skill: Get a ruler and measure these two lines. Reduce fractions of an inch. Put your answers on the lines below the problems.

13. _____

= _____

14. _____

= _____

Work out the following problems. The ones with an asterisk (*) are tricky — the fraction in the answer will be improper, so you will have to change it to a mixed number and then finish the problem.

1. $4 \frac{7}{11}$
   $+3 \frac{1}{11}$
   _____

3. $9 \frac{1}{3}$
   $+7 \frac{1}{3}$
   _____

5. $13 \frac{7}{8}$
   $- 4 \frac{6}{8}$
   _____

7. $8 \frac{4}{5}$ *
   $+3 \frac{3}{5}$
   _____

2. $6 \frac{5}{9}$
   $+2 \frac{2}{9}$
   _____

4. $14 \frac{2}{3}$
   $- 3 \frac{1}{3}$
   _____

6. $16 \frac{5}{8}$
   $+ 3 \frac{2}{8}$
   _____

8. $14 \frac{6}{7}$ *
   $+ 5 \frac{3}{7}$
   _____

Subtracting mixed numbers can also be tricky if the fraction on the top isn't as big as the one on the bottom. Then you have to borrow from the whole number. Borrow one whole and turn it into a fraction.

Example:

$4 \frac{1}{3}$
$-1 \frac{2}{3}$
_____

$4 \frac{1}{3} = 3 \frac{4}{3}$ (Borrow $\frac{3}{3}$ from the 4 and add it to $\frac{1}{3}$.)

$3 \frac{4}{3}$
$-1 \frac{2}{3}$
_____
$2 \frac{2}{3}$ Answer

Practice turning one whole into fractions. Remember: to be one whole, the top and bottom of the fraction should be the same.

Example:

$1 = \frac{8}{8}$

9. $1 = \frac{}{5}$

10. $1 = \frac{}{3}$

11. $1 = \frac{}{2}$

12. $1 = \frac{}{9}$

Try the next two subtraction problems. You will have to borrow from a whole number in each problem.

13. $5 \frac{3}{8}$
    $-1 \frac{5}{8}$
    _____

14. $3 \frac{1}{9}$
    $-1 \frac{5}{9}$
    _____

Measure each of these lines with a ruler. Put your answer on the line to the right. Be sure to reduce fractions of an inch.

15. _____ = ____

16. _____ = ____

17. _____ = ____

18. _____ = ____

19. _____ = ____

20. _____ = ____

Change the following mixed numbers to improper fractions.

1. $5\frac{1}{8}$ = _____

4. $2\frac{3}{4}$ = _____

2. $4\frac{1}{6}$ = _____

5. $6\frac{2}{7}$ = _____

3. $6\frac{1}{9}$ = _____

6. $1\frac{1}{2}$ = _____

Change the following improper fractions to mixed numbers.

7. $\frac{13}{2}$ = _____

10. $\frac{41}{8}$ = _____

8. $\frac{24}{6}$ = _____

11. $\frac{32}{5}$ = _____

9. $\frac{50}{9}$ = _____

12. $\frac{18}{2}$ = _____

Reduce the following fractions to lowest terms.

13. $\frac{6}{12}$ = _____

16. $\frac{9}{12}$ = _____

14. $\frac{4}{16}$ = _____

17. $\frac{7}{35}$ = _____

15. $\frac{18}{20}$ = _____

18. $\frac{30}{32}$ = _____

Write point *B* as a mixed number; be sure to reduce the fraction.

19.

B = _____

20.

B = _____

21. Use a ruler to measure the line below.

_____

= _____

22. Factors of 35 = _____

23. Write 607,000,000,000 in words.

_____

24. $4 : 24 = 7 :$ _____

25. $2 : 12 =$ _____ $: 30$

26. $1135.68 \div 2.8 =$ _____

27. Write MMDXI as an Arabic number.

_____

28. Find the average of 28, 14, 35, and 23.

_____

29. $6.04 \times 9.3 =$ _____

30. $6.4 + 83 + 1.063 =$ _____

31. $9.9 - 1.378 =$ _____

32. Round off 434 to the nearest hundred.

_____

33. Round off .778931 to the nearest hundredth.

_____

34. $4^3 =$ _____

35. Three to the fourth = _____

36. If $\frac{4}{41}$ of a class is absent, what fraction is present?

_____

37. $\frac{6}{7} + \frac{4}{7} =$ _____

38. $\frac{2}{3} - \frac{1}{4} =$ _____

39. $\frac{1}{4} + \frac{2}{5} =$ _____

40. $\dfrac{5}{6} - \dfrac{1}{3} =$ _____

41. Mrs. Twinkle Toes runs 2.9 miles every day, rain or shine. How far would she run during the month of September?

_____

42. Javier did $\dfrac{1}{9}$ of a job, Dai did $\dfrac{1}{5}$, and James did $\dfrac{4}{15}$. How much did they do all together?

_____

43. How much remained to be done?

_____

44. How many feet are in a yard? _____

45. How many cups are in a pint? _____

46. How many quarts are in a gallon? _____

47. How many feet are in a mile? _____

48. How many days are in July? _____

49. How many days are in a leap year? _____

50. How many ounces are in a pound? _____

51. How many pounds are in a ton? _____

Working with Mixed Numbers 3

Work out the following problems. One asterisk (*) means you will have an improper fraction in the answer. Two asterisks (**) mean you will have to borrow from a whole number before you subtract.

1. $3\frac{4}{9}$
    $+5\frac{2}{9}$

5. $7\frac{1}{3}$
    $+8\frac{1}{3}$

9. $16\frac{5}{8}$
    $-2\frac{4}{8}$

13. $6\frac{4}{11}$
    $+8\frac{5}{11}$

2. $9\frac{2}{5}$
    $+8\frac{2}{5}$

6. $16\frac{5}{13}$
    $-4\frac{4}{13}$

10. $8\frac{5}{9}$ *
    $+7\frac{6}{9}$

14. $2\frac{1}{3}$ **
    $-1\frac{2}{3}$

3. $8\frac{3}{5}$
    $-5\frac{1}{5}$

7. $17\frac{3}{7}$
    $+6\frac{2}{7}$

11. $4\frac{1}{5}$
    $+7\frac{1}{5}$

15. $18\frac{7}{8}$ *
    $+11\frac{6}{8}$

4. $3\frac{4}{5}$ *
    $+5\frac{2}{5}$

8. $7\frac{1}{5}$ **
    $-4\frac{3}{5}$

12. $19\frac{5}{11}$
    $+8\frac{5}{11}$

16. $21\frac{4}{5}$
    $-3\frac{1}{5}$

Sometimes you must change a whole number to a mixed number before you can subtract.

Do the following subtraction problems. Make sure the fractions have common denominators.

Example:

$$8 \qquad 7\frac{3}{3}$$
$$-4\frac{2}{3} = -4\frac{2}{3}$$
$$\overline{\qquad} \qquad \overline{3\frac{1}{3}}$$

17. 6
    $-2\frac{1}{7} =$

18. 4
    $-1\frac{3}{4} =$

19. 9
    $-8\frac{1}{2} =$

Measure these lines with a ruler and put your answers on the lines to the right. Reduce fractions of an inch.

20. _____ = ____   22. _____ = ____

21. _____ = ____

Work out the following problems. Watch out for improper fractions — don't leave any in your answers. Also, watch for problems where you have to borrow from a whole number before you subtract.

1. $8 \frac{1}{5}$
   $+7 \frac{3}{5}$

6. $19 \frac{1}{3}$
   $+ 6 \frac{1}{3}$

11. $12 \frac{2}{7}$
    $- 5 \frac{1}{7}$

16. $13 \frac{4}{9}$
    $+ 8 \frac{7}{9}$

2. $14 \frac{1}{8}$
   $+ 9 \frac{4}{8}$

7. $10 \frac{1}{3}$
   $- 4 \frac{2}{3}$

12. $6 \frac{7}{8}$
    $- 5 \frac{2}{8}$

17. 17
    $+18 \frac{3}{10}$

3. $47 \frac{1}{9}$
   $- 6 \frac{3}{9}$

8. 12
   $+ 9 \frac{3}{11}$

13. $14 \frac{3}{5}$
    $+18 \frac{4}{5}$

18. $16 \frac{2}{3}$
    $- 7 \frac{1}{3}$

4. 3
   $-1 \frac{4}{7}$

9. $7 \frac{1}{8}$
   $-4 \frac{1}{8}$

14. $8 \frac{1}{3}$
    $+3 \frac{2}{3}$

19. 6
    $-5 \frac{7}{8}$

5. $18 \frac{4}{5}$
   $- 7 \frac{1}{5}$

10. 10
    $- 1 \frac{1}{9}$

15. $41 \frac{1}{11}$
    $-18 \frac{3}{11}$

20. $59 \frac{2}{3}$
    $+ 8 \frac{2}{3}$

Measure each of these lines with a ruler. Put your answer on the line to the right. Reduce fractions of an inch.

21. _____ = _____   22. _____ = _____

Carefully work out the following problems.

1. $4\dfrac{1}{5}$

    $+\ 8\dfrac{3}{5}$

2. $5\dfrac{2}{5}$

    $+\ 9\dfrac{4}{5}$

3. $9\dfrac{1}{10}$

    $-\ 4\dfrac{3}{10}$

4. 18

    $-\ 9\dfrac{3}{4}$

5. $5\dfrac{4}{9}$

    $-\ 3\dfrac{3}{9}$

6. $4\dfrac{5}{8}$

    $-\ 2\dfrac{1}{3}$

7. 4

    $-\ 2\dfrac{1}{2}$

8. $6\dfrac{1}{3}$

    $-\ 3\dfrac{2}{3}$

9. $2\dfrac{3}{4}$

    $+\ 5\dfrac{1}{4}$

10. $6\dfrac{6}{7}$

    $+\ 9\dfrac{4}{7}$

1. Find the interval, and then figure out what *A* is on the following number line.

```
20                    A      40
|    |    |    |    |    |
```

A = _____

2. Write 290,000,000,000 in words.

_____

3. Factor 90 four ways. _____ _____

_____ _____

4. 48455 ÷ 8 = _____

5. Find the average of 823 and 635.

_____

6. Write four and seventeen thousandths in decimals.

_____

7. 2.375 + 28 + 6.3 = _____

8. 93.6 − 29.463 = _____

9. Round off 354,265 to the nearest thousand.

_____

10. Round off .7764592 to the nearest hundredth.

_____

11. 629 × 2.4 = _____

12. Write MMDCCXLVII in Arabic numbers.

_____

13. 20.976 ÷ .57 = _____

14. 4^3 = _____

15. What fraction of the circle is shaded in?

_____

16. If $\frac{9}{10}$ of a house is painted, how much remains to be done?

_____

17. Complete the ratio.

6 : 36 = _____ : 42

18. $\frac{3}{5} + \frac{1}{8}$ = _____

19. Reduce the following fractions to lowest terms.

$\frac{6}{24}$ = _____ $\frac{9}{12}$ = _____

20. Change $4\frac{3}{5}$ to an improper fraction.

_____

64

To multiply fractions, first multiply the top by the top, then the bottom by the bottom. Check to make sure the answer is reduced to the lowest terms.

Work out the following problems.

Example:

$$\frac{5}{6} \times \frac{3}{5} = \frac{15}{30} = \frac{1}{2}$$

9. $\frac{5}{6} \times \frac{1}{15} = \text{―――} = \text{―――}$

1. $\frac{4}{5} \times \frac{1}{2} = \text{―――} = \text{―――}$

10. $\frac{12}{13} \times \frac{1}{6} = \text{―――} = \text{―――}$

2. $\frac{3}{10} \times \frac{5}{6} = \text{―――} = \text{―――}$

11. $\frac{8}{11}$ of $\frac{2}{3} = \text{―――} = \text{―――}$

3. $\frac{4}{9} \times \frac{6}{7} = \text{―――} = \text{―――}$

12. $\frac{4}{5} \times \frac{15}{16} = \text{―――} = \text{―――}$

4. $\frac{7}{8} \times \frac{4}{11} = \text{―――} = \text{―――}$

13. $\frac{2}{3} \times \frac{9}{10} = \text{―――} = \text{―――}$

5. *of* means "multiply"

$\frac{8}{9}$ of $\frac{3}{4} = \text{―――} = \text{―――}$

14. $\frac{11}{12} \times \frac{6}{7} = \text{―――} = \text{―――}$

6. $\frac{1}{4} \times \frac{8}{9} = \text{―――} = \text{―――}$

15. $\frac{1}{9} \times \frac{3}{4} = \text{―――} = \text{―――}$

7. $\frac{7}{10} \times \frac{5}{14} = \text{―――} = \text{―――}$

16. $\frac{8}{15} \times \frac{3}{4} = \text{―――} = \text{―――}$

8. $\frac{2}{3} \times \frac{6}{7} = \text{―――} = \text{―――}$

17. $\frac{3}{5}$ of $\frac{10}{11} = \text{―――} = \text{―――}$

Sometimes you can cancel before you multiply fractions. This makes the numbers smaller and easier to work with.

To cancel, look diagonally across a problem and see if you can reduce. Then multiply numerators by numerators and denominators by denominators.

Example: $\dfrac{7}{\cancel{9}_3} \times \dfrac{\cancel{3}^1}{4} = \dfrac{7}{3} \times \dfrac{1}{4} = \dfrac{7}{12}$

Study the next example and do the rest of the problems.

1. $\dfrac{\cancel{5}^1}{\cancel{6}_2} \times \dfrac{\cancel{3}^1}{\cancel{5}_1} =$ ——

4. $\dfrac{1}{2} \times \dfrac{4}{5} =$ ——

7. $\dfrac{12}{13} \times \dfrac{1}{6} =$ ——

10. $\dfrac{4}{5}$ of $\dfrac{20}{21} =$ ——

2. $\dfrac{4}{9} \times \dfrac{12}{13} =$ ——

5. $\dfrac{2}{3} \times \dfrac{9}{10} =$ ——

8. $\dfrac{2}{3} \times \dfrac{15}{16} =$ ——

11. $\dfrac{3}{7} \times \dfrac{7}{24} =$ ——

3. $\dfrac{2}{8}$ of $\dfrac{4}{5} =$ ——

6. $\dfrac{5}{7}$ of $\dfrac{7}{10} =$ ——

9. $\dfrac{9}{11}$ of $\dfrac{2}{3} =$ ——

Cancel if you can and then multiply. If you come across a whole number, make it into a fraction by putting it over 1.

Example:
$13 = \dfrac{13}{1}$

12. $\dfrac{3}{4} \times \dfrac{12}{15} =$ ——

15. $\dfrac{1}{2} \times 12 =$ ——

18. $\dfrac{5}{6}$ of $\dfrac{9}{10} =$ ——

13. $\dfrac{2}{3} \times \dfrac{3}{18} =$ ——

16. $\dfrac{4}{9}$ of $\dfrac{7}{8} =$ ——

19. $\dfrac{4}{7} \times \dfrac{2}{5} =$ ——

14. $\dfrac{3}{8}$ of $16 =$ ——

17. $\dfrac{2}{3} \times \dfrac{5}{7} =$ ——

20. $\dfrac{4}{7}$ of $14 =$ ——

Review 27

46

Change the following mixed numbers to improper fractions.

1. $2\frac{1}{8}$ =_____

2. $4\frac{1}{5}$ =_____

3. $1\frac{1}{8}$ =_____

4. $3\frac{5}{6}$ =_____

5. $5\frac{1}{9}$ =_____

6. $10\frac{2}{3}$ =_____

Change the following improper fractions to mixed numbers. Reduce your answers to lowest terms.

7. $\frac{13}{2}$ =_____

8. $\frac{20}{3}$ =_____

9. $\frac{45}{6}$ =_____

10. $\frac{14}{7}$ =_____

11. $\frac{14}{5}$ =_____

12. $\frac{29}{8}$ =_____

13. $\begin{array}{r} 4\frac{4}{5} \\ +5\frac{4}{5} \\ \hline \end{array}$

14. $\begin{array}{r} 6\frac{1}{3} \\ -4\frac{2}{3} \\ \hline \end{array}$

15. $\begin{array}{r} 5\frac{1}{9} \\ +6\frac{8}{9} \\ \hline \end{array}$

16. $\begin{array}{r} 6\frac{1}{9} \\ -1\frac{2}{9} \\ \hline \end{array}$

17. Write point A as a mixed number. Reduce your answer to lowest terms.

3   A   4

A =_____

18. Factors of 50 =_____ _____

19. Write twenty-one billion in numbers.

_____

20. 6 : 72 = 8: _____

21. 164.84 ÷ 2.6 = _____

22. Find the average of 99 and 103.

_____

23. 43.51 × .73 = _____

24. Write 21.016 in words.

_____

_____

25. 8.3 + 21 + 36.94 =_____

26. 18.9 − 9.314 = _____

27. Circle the measures used for weight.
    centimeters
    inches
    pounds
    miles
    ounces
    grams
    millimeters
    kilograms
    tons
    liters

28. Round off 561 to the nearest hundred.

_____

29. Round off .743294 to the nearest thousandth.

_____

30. Write 2,498 in Roman numerals.

_____

31. Four cubed + five squared = _____

32. Figure out what B is on the following number line.

14   B   32

B =_____

67

Reduce to lowest terms.

33. $\dfrac{9}{27}$ = _____

34. $\dfrac{18}{24}$ = _____

35. $\dfrac{4}{7} + \dfrac{5}{7}$ = _____

36. $\dfrac{6}{7} - \dfrac{2}{5}$ = _____

37. $\dfrac{3}{4} + \dfrac{1}{5}$ = _____

38. DeShonda earns $11,220 in four months. How much does she earn each month?

_____

39. Vibha weighs 37 pounds. Her mother weighs four times that much. How much does her mother weigh?

_____

40. Circle the metric measure you would use to weigh an elephant.
    milligrams
    grams
    kilograms

41. Which metric measure would you use to weigh a pencil?

_____

Work out the following multiplication problems. First, change the mixed numbers to improper fractions; then cancel if you can. Make sure the answer is reduced to lowest terms.

Example:

$$1\frac{3}{4} \times 2\frac{4}{7} = \frac{\cancel{7}^{1}}{\cancel{4}_{2}} \times \frac{\cancel{18}^{9}}{\cancel{7}_{1}} = \frac{9}{2} = 4\frac{1}{2}$$

1. $3\frac{1}{4} \times 4\frac{4}{5} =$

   $\frac{13}{4} \times \frac{24}{5} =$ _____

2. $5\frac{1}{2} \times 3\frac{6}{11} =$ _____

3. $\frac{3}{4} \times 1\frac{1}{3} =$ _____

4. $4\frac{1}{5} \times 5 =$ _____

5. $8\frac{1}{3} \times 6\frac{2}{5} =$ _____

6. $6\frac{2}{3} \times 2\frac{1}{10} =$ _____

7. $1\frac{1}{2} \times 1\frac{6}{7} =$ _____

8. $2\frac{1}{4} \times 1\frac{1}{9} =$ _____

Now work out the following multiplication problems. Make sure the answer is reduced to lowest terms.

9. $\frac{2}{3} \times 4\frac{1}{2} =$ _____

10. $\frac{1}{7} \times 15 =$ _____

11. $6\frac{1}{8} \times \frac{5}{7} =$ _____

12. $\frac{2}{3} \times \frac{5}{16} =$ _____

13. $8\frac{1}{8} \times 8 =$ _____

Now do these problems.

14. If it takes $1\frac{3}{4}$ yards of fabric to make 1 dress, how much fabric is needed to make 8 dresses?

_____

15. The distance around a running track is $\frac{1}{4}$ of a mile. If you run around the track 14 times, how many miles will you run?

_____

Do the following multiplication problems. Reduce the answers to lowest terms.

1. $\dfrac{8}{9} \times 3\dfrac{3}{4}$ = _____

2. $4\dfrac{2}{5} \times 1\dfrac{7}{8}$ = _____

3. $\dfrac{4}{5}$ of $\dfrac{9}{10}$ = _____

4. $2\dfrac{5}{9} \times \dfrac{3}{4}$ = _____

5. $\dfrac{1}{8}$ of 12 = _____

6. $\dfrac{2}{9} \times \dfrac{3}{4}$ = _____

7. $2\dfrac{1}{5} \times 4\dfrac{3}{8}$ = _____

8. $\dfrac{4}{7} \times \dfrac{14}{15}$ = _____

9. $\dfrac{11}{12} \times 6\dfrac{3}{4}$ = _____

10. $1\dfrac{3}{13} \times 4\dfrac{1}{6}$ = _____

11. $\dfrac{2}{7} \times 28$ = _____

12. $2\dfrac{4}{9} \times \dfrac{18}{19}$ = _____

13. $\dfrac{3}{4}$ of $\dfrac{2}{7}$ = _____

14. $\dfrac{1}{2} \times 6$ = _____

15. $\dfrac{7}{8} \times \dfrac{2}{7}$ = _____

16. $\dfrac{3}{8}$ of $\dfrac{5}{7}$ = _____

17. $\dfrac{9}{10}$ of 30 = _____

18. $\dfrac{1}{2} \times 2\dfrac{14}{15}$ = _____

19. $6\dfrac{2}{3} \times 8\dfrac{1}{10}$ = _____

20. $\dfrac{4}{9}$ of $2\dfrac{2}{3}$ = _____

21. $\dfrac{1}{4}$ of 12 = _____

Now do these problems.

22. It takes $1\dfrac{3}{4}$ cups of sugar to make a batch of chocolate chip cookies. How much sugar is needed to make 4 batches of cookies?

_____

23. Uncle Frank wants to give $2.50 ($2\dfrac{1}{2}$ dollars) to each of his 10 nephews and nieces for Christmas. How much money will he be giving all together?

_____

Do the following multiplication problems. Make sure each answer is reduced to the lowest terms.

1. $\dfrac{2}{3} \times \dfrac{3}{4} =$ _____

2. $\dfrac{3}{10} \times \dfrac{5}{6} =$ _____

3. $\dfrac{4}{5} \times \dfrac{3}{8} =$ _____

4. $\dfrac{9}{11}$ of $33 =$ _____

5. $\dfrac{4}{5}$ of $20 =$ _____

6. $\dfrac{7}{8}$ of $\dfrac{4}{5} =$ _____

7. $1\dfrac{2}{3} \times 6\dfrac{1}{2} =$ _____

8. $4\dfrac{1}{5} \times 2\dfrac{3}{4} =$ _____

9. $9\dfrac{1}{2} \times 1\dfrac{2}{5} =$ _____

10. $7\dfrac{3}{4} \times 2\dfrac{5}{6} =$ _____

1. Figure out what *A* is on the following number line.

```
   18                    A      22
   |    |    |    |    |    |
```

A = _____

2. Write four hundred thirty-five million in numbers.

_____

3. Factor 40 three ways. _____

_____   _____

4. 65754 ÷ 8 = _____

5. Find the average of 10, 12, 16, 13, and 19.

_____

6. Write 8.13 in words.

_____

7. 4.589 + 35 + 1.8 = _____

8. 75.8 − 28.5 = _____

9. Round off 372,586,211 to the nearest million.

_____

10. Round off .42837941 to the nearest thousandth.

_____

11. 2.71 × 3.8 = _____

12. Write 3,947 in Roman numerals.

_____

13. 300.94 ÷ 8.2 = _____

14. Five cubed = _____

15. What fraction of the circle is shaded in?

_____

16. If $\frac{14}{17}$ of a class is men, what fraction is women?

_____

17. Complete the ratio.

4 : 36 = 5 : _____

18. $\frac{5}{6} - \frac{2}{9}$ = _____

19. Reduce the following fractions to lowest terms.

$\frac{3}{35}$ = _____ $\frac{14}{16}$ = _____

20. Change $2\frac{5}{9}$ to an improper fraction.

_____

21. $7\frac{5}{7}$
    $+8\frac{6}{7}$
    _____

22. $5\frac{1}{3}$
    $-2\frac{2}{3}$
    _____

23. Write point *B* as a mixed number. Reduce your answer to the lowest terms.

```
   3         B                      4
   |   |   |   |   |   |   |   |   |   |
```

B = _____

Once you know how to multiply fractions and mixed numbers, dividing them is easy. Just turn the second fraction upside down and multiply. Cancel if you can, but make sure you don't cancel until the second fraction is turned upside down.

Example:

$$\frac{2}{7} \div \frac{11}{14} = \frac{2}{7} \times \frac{14}{11} \rightarrow \quad \text{now cancel and then multiply} \quad \rightarrow \frac{2}{\cancel{7}_1} \times \frac{\cancel{14}^2}{11} = \frac{4}{11} \text{ Answer}$$

copy — turn upside down

Now try the following problems.

1. $\frac{2}{9} \div \frac{2}{3} =$ _____ × _____ = _____

2. $\frac{3}{10} \div \frac{4}{5} =$ _____ × _____ = _____

3. $\frac{1}{8} \div \frac{2}{3} =$ _____ × _____ = _____

4. $\frac{4}{7} \div \frac{5}{7} =$ _____ × _____ = _____

5. $\frac{2}{5} \div \frac{7}{10} =$ _____ × _____ = _____

6. $\frac{6}{7} \div \frac{12}{13} =$ _____ × _____ = _____

7. $\frac{2}{15} \div \frac{4}{5} =$ _____ × _____ = _____

8. $\frac{5}{12} \div \frac{5}{6} =$ _____ × _____ = _____

9. $\frac{5}{6} \div \frac{7}{8} =$ _____ × _____ = _____

10. $\frac{1}{3} \div \frac{4}{5} =$ _____ × _____ = _____

11. $\frac{2}{15} \div \frac{2}{5} =$ _____ × _____ = _____

12. $\frac{4}{11} \div \frac{9}{22} =$ _____ × _____ = _____

To divide fractions, turn the second fraction upside down, cancel if you can, and multiply.

Do the following problems. If any of the answers are improper (top heavy), change them to mixed numbers.

1. $\dfrac{3}{8} \div \dfrac{3}{4} =$ _____ × _____ = _____

2. $\dfrac{4}{7} \div \dfrac{1}{28} =$ _____ × _____ = _____

3. $\dfrac{2}{9} \div \dfrac{18}{27} =$ _____

4. $\dfrac{3}{5} \div \dfrac{17}{20} =$ _____

5. $\dfrac{6}{7} \div \dfrac{13}{14} =$ _____

6. $\dfrac{2}{11} \div \dfrac{20}{33} =$ _____

7. $\dfrac{9}{13} \div \dfrac{12}{13} =$ _____

8. $\dfrac{5}{21} \div \dfrac{5}{7} =$ _____

Work out the following problems. First change the mixed numbers to improper fractions; then divide. Cancel if you can.

Example:

$$3\dfrac{1}{3} \div 4\dfrac{4}{9} = \dfrac{10}{3} \div \dfrac{40}{9} = \dfrac{\cancel{10}^{1}}{\cancel{3}_{1}} \times \dfrac{\cancel{9}^{3}}{\cancel{40}_{4}} = \dfrac{3}{4} \text{ Answer}$$

9. $2\dfrac{1}{2} \div 3\dfrac{3}{4} =$ _____ ÷ _____ = _____ × _____ = _____

10. $6\dfrac{1}{8} \div 7\dfrac{7}{10} =$ _____

11. $1\dfrac{1}{2} \div 2\dfrac{3}{4} =$ _____

12. $\dfrac{2}{3} \div 1\dfrac{1}{3} =$ _____

13. $4\dfrac{1}{6} \div 7\dfrac{1}{7} =$ _____

14. $3\dfrac{2}{3} \div 5\dfrac{1}{2} =$ _____

15. $8\dfrac{4}{7} \div 11\dfrac{3}{7} =$ _____

1. $1\frac{2}{3} \times 3\frac{1}{4} =$ _____

2. $\frac{4}{5} \times 2\frac{1}{8} =$ _____

3. $4\frac{3}{4} \times \frac{4}{19} =$ _____

4. $2\frac{2}{3} \times 4\frac{1}{4} =$ _____

5. $\frac{3}{4} \times \frac{4}{5} =$ _____

6. $\frac{8}{9}$ of 45 = _____

7. Use a ruler to measure the line.

_____

= _____

Reduce the following to lowest terms.

8. $\frac{4}{20} =$ _____   9. $\frac{12}{16} =$ _____

10. $\begin{array}{r} 7\frac{1}{7} \\ -2\frac{4}{7} \\ \hline \end{array}$ 11. $\begin{array}{r} 6\frac{3}{5} \\ +7\frac{4}{5} \\ \hline \end{array}$

12. Write $5\frac{3}{5}$ as an improper fraction.

_____

13. If $\frac{4}{10}$ of the pie has been eaten, how much is left? _____

14. $\frac{4}{7} + \frac{5}{7} =$ _____

15. $\frac{8}{9} - \frac{1}{6} =$ _____

16. $\frac{2}{3} + \frac{1}{8} =$ _____

17. $2^5 =$ _____

18. Ten squared = _____

19. $151.536 \div .42 =$ _____

20. $19.8 \times .53 =$ _____

21. Write CMLXXVI as an Arabic number.

_____

22. Find the average of 75 and 83.

_____

23. Round off .4738921 to the nearest thousandth.

_____

24. Round off 749 to the nearest hundred.

_____

25. $84.3 + 2.73 + 11 =$ _____

26. $80.5 - 21.413 =$ _____

27. Write two and seventeen hundredths in decimals.

_____

28. Write 908,000,000,000 in words.

_____

29. A jet fighter goes 1,258 miles an hour. How far can it go in 5 hours at this speed?

_____

30. A new car gets 15 miles to the gallon. There are 12.8 gallons left in the tank, and 194 miles to the nearest gas station. Will the car make it to the station?

_____

31. Circle the best metric measure for your weight.
      milligram
      gram
      kilogram

32. Circle the metric measure you would use to measure milk for a cake mix.
      milliliter
      liter

33. Circle the metric measure you would use to measure the length of a classroom.
    - millimeter
    - centimeter
    - meter
    - kilometer

34. How many seconds are in a minute? _____

35. How many hours are in a day? _____

36. How many quarts are in a gallon? _____

37. How many years are in a decade? _____

38. How many years are in a century? _____

39. How many cents are in a quarter? _____

Work out the following problems. If any of the answers are improper, change them to mixed numbers.

1. $\frac{3}{7} \div \frac{9}{14}$ = _____

2. $5\frac{4}{5} \div 6\frac{1}{10}$ = _____

3. $3\frac{3}{10} \div 6\frac{3}{5}$ = _____

4. $\frac{5}{6} \div \frac{9}{14}$ = _____

5. $12 \div \frac{6}{7}$ = _____

6. $\frac{5}{6} \div \frac{12}{13}$ = _____

7. $2\frac{1}{4} \div \frac{3}{4}$ = _____

8. $8\frac{4}{7} \div 2\frac{1}{7}$ = _____

9. $\frac{2}{9} \div \frac{5}{6}$ = _____

10. $10 \div \frac{3}{4}$ = _____

11. $9\frac{1}{3} \div 1\frac{1}{6}$ = _____

12. $\frac{4}{11} \div \frac{21}{22}$ = _____

13. $16 \div \frac{1}{2}$ = _____

14. $4\frac{3}{4} \div 9\frac{1}{2}$ = _____

Dividing Fractions and Mixed Numbers 4

Work out the following problems. Be careful—some are division problems, and some are multiplication problems.

1. $10 \div 2\frac{1}{4} =$ _____

2. $\frac{4}{21} \div \frac{11}{14} =$ _____

3. $1\frac{6}{7} \div 3\frac{5}{7} =$ _____

4. $18 \times 2\frac{1}{6} =$ _____

5. $\frac{2}{9} \div \frac{11}{12} =$ _____

6. $1\frac{2}{9} \times \frac{2}{11} =$ _____

7. $6\frac{3}{7} \div \frac{9}{14} =$ _____

8. $4\frac{1}{5} \div 2\frac{7}{10} =$ _____

9. $8 \div \frac{1}{4} =$ _____

10. $\frac{2}{3} \div \frac{1}{3} =$ _____

11. $15 \div \frac{1}{2} =$ _____

12. $3\frac{3}{4} \times \frac{4}{5} =$ _____

13. $8\frac{1}{3} \div 2\frac{2}{9} =$ _____

14. $9\frac{2}{7} \div \frac{5}{7} =$ _____

Work out the following problems. Make sure the answers are reduced to the lowest terms and, if necessary, turned into mixed numbers.

1. $\dfrac{6}{11} \div \dfrac{21}{22} =$ _____

2. $\dfrac{7}{8} \div 14 =$ _____

3. $\dfrac{8}{9} \div \dfrac{1}{12} =$ _____

4. $\dfrac{5}{13} \div \dfrac{10}{11} =$ _____

5. $\dfrac{3}{5} \div 2\dfrac{1}{4} =$ _____

6. $\dfrac{2}{9} \div \dfrac{10}{27} =$ _____

7. $12 \div \dfrac{4}{5} =$ _____

8. $2\dfrac{1}{2} \div 4\dfrac{2}{3} =$ _____

9. $1\dfrac{1}{3} \div \dfrac{2}{5} =$ _____

10. $\dfrac{3}{8} \div 42 =$ _____

1. Find out what *A* is on the following number line.

   21   A   49

   A = _____

2. Write 922,000,000,000,000 in words.

   _____

   _____

3. Factor 60 four ways. _____   _____

   _____   _____

4. 48218 ÷ 8 = _____

5. Find the average of 822 and 900.

   _____

6. Write twelve and seven thousandths in decimals.

   _____

7. 509 + 2.7 + 1.35 = _____

8. 63.2 − 45.189 = _____

9. Round off 735,981 to the nearest thousand.

   _____

10. Round off 76.479315 to the nearest tenth.

    _____

11. 685 × .23 = _____

12. Write MMMDCXLIV in Arabic numbers.

    _____

13. 105.57 ÷ 2.7 = _____

14. 4^4 = _____

15. What fraction of the circle is shaded in?

    _____

16. If $\dfrac{17}{20}$ of a test is wrong, what fraction is right?

    _____

17. Complete the ratio.

    5 : 40 = _____ : 56

18. $\dfrac{3}{8} + \dfrac{1}{3}$ = _____

19. Reduce the following fractions to lowest terms.

    $\dfrac{8}{40}$ = _____ $\dfrac{15}{20}$ = _____

20. Change $7\dfrac{1}{3}$ to an improper fraction.

    _____

21. $\begin{aligned} &9\dfrac{8}{9} \\ +\,&1\dfrac{5}{9} \end{aligned}$

    ‾‾‾‾‾‾

22. $\begin{aligned} &4\dfrac{2}{7} \\ -\,&2\dfrac{4}{7} \end{aligned}$

    ‾‾‾‾‾‾

23. Write point *B* as a mixed number. Reduce your answer to lowest terms.

    7   B   8

    B = _____

24. $\dfrac{3}{8}$ of 24 = _____

A *percent sign* is made like this: %. *Percent* means "hundredths" or "out of one hundred," so 23% is the same as .23 and $\frac{23}{100}$. 8% is the same as .08 and $\frac{8}{100}$.

Write the following percents as decimals and as fractions.

1. 45% = .____ = $\frac{\quad}{100}$

2. 99% = ____ = ____

3. 21% = ____ = ____

4. 78% = ____ = ____

5. 33% = ____ = ____

6. 87% = ____ = ____

Write the following fractions as decimals and then as percents.

7. $\frac{13}{100}$ = .____ = ____ %

8. $\frac{45}{100}$ = ____ = ____

9. $\frac{25}{100}$ = ____ = ____

10. $\frac{75}{100}$ = ____ = ____

11. $\frac{50}{100}$ = ____ = ____

12. $\frac{90}{100}$ = ____ = ____

Any fraction can be changed to a percent. But first you must change it to a decimal.

To change a fraction to a decimal, divide the bottom of the fraction into the top. Add a decimal point and two zeroes.

Example:

Fraction

$$\frac{1}{4} \rightarrow \begin{array}{r} .25 \\ 4\overline{)1.00} \\ \underline{8} \\ 20 \\ \underline{20} \\ 00 \end{array}$$

$\frac{1}{4}$ = .25

To change the decimal to a percent, move the decimal point two places to the right and add the percent sign (%).

Example:

Decimal   Percent

.25   →   .25   =   25%

Note that everything to the left of the decimal is a whole number, so 25. and 25 are the same.

Change the following fractions first to decimals and then to percents.

	Fraction	Decimal	Percent		Fraction	Decimal	Percent
13.	$\frac{3}{4}$ =	____ =	_____	15.	$\frac{1}{2}$ =	____ =	_____
14.	$\frac{4}{5}$ =	____ =	_____	16.	$\frac{3}{5}$ =	____ =	_____

Change each of the following fractions to a decimal; then change the decimal to a percent.

Example:

Fraction		Decimal	Percent
$\frac{1}{4} =$	$\begin{array}{r} .25 \\ 4\overline{)1.00} \\ \underline{8} \\ 20 \\ \underline{20} \end{array}$	.25	25%

An asterisk (*) after a fraction means there will be a remainder when you divide to the hundredths place. Write the remainder as a fraction, move the decimal over two places to the right, and add the percent sign.

Example:

Fraction		Decimal	Percent
$\frac{1}{3}$ * $=$	$\begin{array}{r} .33 \\ 3\overline{)1.00} \\ \underline{9} \\ 10 \\ \underline{9} \\ \frac{1}{3} \end{array}$	$.33\frac{1}{3}$	$33\frac{1}{3}$ %

	Fraction	Decimal	Percent		Fraction	Decimal	Percent
1.	$\frac{1}{2}$			6.	$\frac{1}{8}$ *		
2.	$\frac{2}{5}$			7.	$\frac{3}{8}$ *		
3.	$\frac{3}{4}$			8.	$\frac{5}{8}$ *		
4.	$\frac{2}{3}$ *			9.	$\frac{7}{8}$ *		
5.	$\frac{3}{10}$			10.	$\frac{5}{5}$		

1. $\frac{4}{9} \div \frac{5}{6} =$ _____

2. $\frac{4}{11} \div \frac{15}{22} =$ _____

3. $2\frac{1}{8} \div 5\frac{2}{3} =$ _____

4. $5\frac{2}{5} \div \frac{11}{15} =$ _____

5. $\frac{6}{7} \times 1\frac{1}{6} =$ _____

6. $3\frac{1}{8} \times 0 =$ _____

7. $\frac{9}{10} \times 2\frac{1}{7} =$ _____

8. $8\frac{1}{3} \div 4\frac{1}{6} =$ _____

9. $\frac{3}{4} \div \frac{15}{16} =$ _____

10. $\frac{2}{9}$ of 81 = _____

11. $\frac{9}{10} \times \frac{2}{3} =$ _____

12. Use a ruler to measure this line.

_____

= _____

Reduce the following to the lowest terms.

13. $\frac{14}{20} =$ _____   14. $\frac{9}{81} =$ _____

15. Write $9\frac{1}{7}$ as an improper fraction.

_____

16. $\frac{2}{3} + \frac{2}{3} =$ _____

17. $\frac{9}{10} - \frac{2}{3} =$ _____

18. $\frac{2}{5} + \frac{3}{8} =$ _____

19. Two to the fifth = _____

20. $9^2 =$ _____

21. $14.906 - .58 =$ _____

22. $37.9 \times 41 =$ _____

23. Write 1,029 in Roman numerals.

_____

24. Find the average of 88, 39, and 41.

_____

25. $18.6 + 2.971 =$ _____

26. $68 - 2.47 =$ _____

27. Round off 4.93841 to the nearest hundredth.

_____

28. Round off 57,358 to the nearest thousand.

_____

29. Write 46.019 in words.

_____

30. Circle the measures of distance.
    millimeters
    inches
    gallons
    tons
    miles
    kilometers
    centimeters
    yards
    cups
    liters
    grams

31. Circle the metric measure you would use to weigh a feather.
    milligram
    gram
    kilogram

32. Circle the metric measure you would use to measure the distance from Boston to New York.

    millimeter
    centimeter
    meter
    kilometer

33. How many quarts are in 4 gallons? _____

34. How many feet are in a mile? _____

35. How many days are in May? _____

36. Mr. Glenroy and his wife and three children went to a movie. All the children were over 12 and had to pay the full price. All the tickets together cost $37.50. How much did each ticket cost?

    _____

37. A Roman woman lived from the year CXXXVI until CCXIV. How old was she when she died? Answer in Arabic numbers.

    _____

Fill in the table below by finding fractions, decimals, and percents.

	Fraction	Decimal	Percent
	$\frac{1}{4}$	.25	25%
1.	$\frac{3}{4}$		
2.	$\frac{1}{2}$		
3.	$\frac{1}{3}$		
4.	$\frac{2}{3}$		

Be sure to reduce these fractions to the lowest terms.

	Fraction	Decimal	Percent
5.		.20	
6.		.40	
7.		.60	
8.		.80	

	Fraction	Decimal	Percent
9.			90%
10.			10%
11.			5%
12.			15%

Work these out to the hundredths place and include the remainder as a fraction in the decimal and in the percent.

	Fraction	Decimal	Percent
	$\frac{1}{8}$	$.12\frac{1}{2}$	$12\frac{1}{2}\%$
13.	$\frac{3}{8}$		
14.	$\frac{5}{8}$		
15.	$\frac{7}{8}$		

	Fraction	Decimal	Percent
16.	$\frac{8}{8}$		
17.	$\frac{7}{20}$		
18.	$\frac{9}{20}$		

Solve the following two word problems.

19. A baseball player got 3 hits out of 8 times at bat. What is his batting average as a decimal?

_____

20. What percent of the time did he hit?

_____

Fractions, Decimals, and Percent 4

Fill in the table below by finding fractions, decimals, and percents. If you have a remainder after dividing to the hundredths place, leave it as a fraction and include it in the decimal and in the percent. Remember to reduce the fractions to the lowest terms.

	Fraction	Decimal	Percent			Fraction	Decimal	Percent
1.		.50			11.		.99	
2.	$\frac{1}{4}$				12.		.01	
3.			75%		13.			30%
4.	$\frac{1}{3}$				14.	$\frac{1}{8}$		
5.	$\frac{2}{3}$				15.	$\frac{3}{8}$		
6.			100%		16.	$\frac{5}{8}$		
7.	$\frac{1}{5}$				17.	$\frac{7}{8}$		
8.	$\frac{2}{5}$				18.			55%
9.	$\frac{3}{5}$				19.	$\frac{9}{10}$		
10.			80%		20.		.70	

Now see if you can solve the two word problems below.

21. A baseball player gets 7 hits out of 26 times at bat. What is her batting average? (Divide to the ten-thousandths place and round off to the nearest thousandth.)

_____

22. What percent of the time did she hit?

_____

Fill in the table with the equivalent fractions, decimals, and percents. If you have a remainder after dividing to the hundredths place, leave it as a fraction and include it in the decimal and in the percent. Remember when finding the fraction to reduce it to the lowest terms.

	Fraction	Decimal	Percent
1.	$\frac{1}{4}$		
2.	$\frac{3}{8}$		
3.	$\frac{4}{5}$		
4.	$\frac{1}{3}$		
5.	$\frac{9}{10}$		
6.		.75	
7.			$66\frac{2}{3}\%$
8.			40%
9.			10%
10.		.59	

1. Figure out what *A* is on the following number line.

18   A   26

A = _____

2. Write five hundred thousand in numbers.

_____

3. Factor 88 three ways. _____

_____   _____

4. 21398 ÷ 7 = _____

5. Find the average of 19, 23, and 15.

_____

6. Write 6.11 in words.

_____

7. 28.491 + 3.66 + 88 = _____

8. 47.3 − 29.115 = _____

9. Round off 681,499,216 to the nearest million.

_____

10. Round off 88.935711 to the nearest one.

_____

11. 8.39 × .62 = _____

12. Write 2,389 in Roman numerals.

_____

13. 26.372 ÷ .38 = _____

14. Three cubed = _____

15. What fraction of the circle is shaded in?

_____

16. If $\dfrac{13}{15}$ of a hotel is filled, what fraction is empty?

_____

17. Complete the ratio.

9 : 54 = 10 : _____

18. $\dfrac{9}{10} - \dfrac{2}{3} =$ _____

19. Reduce the following fractions to lowest terms.

$\dfrac{6}{24} =$ _____ $\dfrac{20}{22} =$ _____

20. Change $6\dfrac{2}{3}$ to an improper fraction.

_____

21. $4\dfrac{3}{5}$
$+4\dfrac{3}{5}$

22. $5\dfrac{1}{9}$
$-2\dfrac{3}{9}$

23. Write point *B* as a mixed number. Reduce your answer to lowest terms.

8   B   9

B = _____

24. $4\dfrac{5}{6} \times 2\dfrac{9}{10} =$ _____

25. $\dfrac{1}{7} \div \dfrac{16}{21} =$ _____

Percent means "hundredths." To find the percent of something, you change the percent to a decimal and multiply.

Example:

25% of 83 =

.25 × 83 =

$$\begin{array}{r} 83 \\ \times.25 \\ \hline 415 \\ 166 \\ \hline 20.75 \text{ Answer} \end{array}$$

Work out the following problems.

1. 25% of 145 = _____

2. 18% of 64 = _____

3. 99% of 200 = _____

4. 65% of 128 = _____

5. 50% of 44 = _____
   (Can you think of a short cut for this one?)

6. 75% of 88 = _____

7. 5% of 64 = _____
   (Remember to add the zero.)

8. 12% of 214 = _____

9. 49% of 1000 = _____

10. 2% of 215 = _____
    (Remember to add the zero.)

Now solve this word problem.

11. A woman made $45,000 a year. She had to pay 32% of that in taxes. How much was her tax bill?

_____

Remember: to find the percent of something, change the percent to a decimal and then multiply.

Work out the following percent problems.

1. 25% of 200 = .25 × 200 = _____

2. 78% of 423 = _____

3. 7% of 2,000 = _____

4. 18% of 25 = _____

5. 99% of 100 = _____

6. 50% of 94 = _____

100% is all of something. It is 1.00 or 1. or one whole. More than 100% is more than 1.00 or more than one whole. 135% is 1.35 or one whole and $\frac{35}{100}$

Write the following percents first as whole numbers and decimals and then as mixed numbers.

7. 178% = _____ 1.78 _____ = _____

8. 112% = _____ = _____

9. 199% = _____ = _____

10. 225% = _____ = _____

11. 342% = _____ = _____

12. 500% = _____ = _____

Some percents like 37.5% or 66.7% are not exact hundredths. As you can see, these percents have decimal points in them. To change these percents to decimals, move the decimal point two places to the left. You may have to add a zero to do this.

Change the following percents to decimals.

Examples:

37.5% = .375   7.5% = .075

13. 66.7% = _____

14. 62.5% = _____

15. 33.3% = _____

16. 3.1% = _____

17. 4.91% = _____

18. 77.01% = _____

19. 125.3% = _____

Using what you have learned in the instructions above, carefully work out the following problems.

20. 125% of 60 = _____

21. 150% of 212 = _____

22. 33.3% of 85 = _____

23. 29% of 63 = _____

24. 175% of 18 = _____

25. 215% of 69 = _____

26. 87.5% of 72 = _____

27. 4.5% of 900 = _____

Review 30

Write the following percents as fractions.

1. $90\% =$ _____

2. $25\% =$ _____

3. $80\% =$ _____

4. $66\frac{2}{3}\% =$ _____

Write the following fractions as percents.

5. $\frac{1}{2} =$ _____

6. $\frac{1}{3} =$ _____

7. $\frac{1}{4} =$ _____

8. $\frac{1}{8} =$ _____

9. $\frac{5}{8} =$ _____

10. $\frac{1}{5} =$ _____

11. $\frac{9}{9} =$ _____

12. $\frac{1}{3}$ of 18 = _____

Reduce the following fractions to lowest terms.

13. $\frac{9}{45} =$ _____

14. $\frac{4}{6} =$ _____

15. $\frac{7}{8} \div \frac{1}{2} =$ _____

16. Use a ruler to measure the line.

_____ = _____

17. $7\frac{2}{3}$
   $+4\frac{1}{3}$
   _____

18. $8\frac{1}{5}$
   $-1\frac{2}{5}$
   _____

19. Write $6\frac{2}{5}$ as an improper fraction.

_____

20. $\frac{1}{5} + \frac{2}{3} =$ _____

21. $\frac{6}{7} + \frac{4}{7} =$ _____

22. $7^3 =$ _____

23. Nine cubed = _____

24. $95.004 \div 6.3 =$ _____

25. $2.08 \times .78 =$ _____

26. Write 2,478 in Roman numerals.

_____

27. Round off .98473718 to the nearest hundredth.

_____

28. Round off 18 to the nearest ten.

_____

29. $4.831 + 1.2 + 47 =$ _____

30. $9 - 2.87 =$ _____

31. Write fourteen and eight thousandths in decimals.

_____

32. Write 318,000,000 in words.

_____

33. How many feet are in a mile? _____

34. How many days are in a year? _____

35. How many pounds are in a ton? _____

36. How many quarts are in a gallon? _____

37. How many seconds are in five minutes?

_____

38. Charlie wants to save a thousand dollars. He can save $5 a week. How many weeks will it take him to reach his goal?

_____

39. About how many years is that, if there are 52 weeks in a year?

_____

40. Mr. Gleason weighs 573 pounds. In March he loses 15.8 pounds; in April he loses 19.6 pounds; and in May he loses 14.5 pounds. Then in June he gains back 2.4 pounds. What does he weigh at the end of June?

_____

Percent 3

Change the following percents to decimals.

1. 55% = _____

2. 67% = _____

3. 9% = _____

4. 73.1% = _____

5. 2% = _____

6. 125% = _____

7. 64% = _____

8. 7.3% = _____

9. 294% = _____

Now work out the following word problems. Remember: change the percent to a decimal and multiply.

10. 60% of the children in a class of 25 are girls. How many girls are there?

11. A man puts $600 in a bank. The bank pays him 5% interest on that money each year. How much interest does the man make in one year?

12. A boy took a test with 25 questions and got 80% right. How many did he get right?

13. 200,000 people voted in an election. The winning candidate got 55% of the votes. How many votes did she get?

14. A school has 900 students. It is 35% Black. How many Black students are there?

Percent also means "out of a hundred." Subtract the percent from one hundred percent to answer the following questions.

15. 25% of a tank of gasoline is used up. What percent is left?

16. 99% of the people in a city are television owners. What percent is not?

17. 6% of the cars in a parking lot are foreign cars. What percent are not foreign?

18. 54% of the children in a class are girls. What percent of the students are boys?

Carefully work out the following problems. If an answer calls for a decimal point, don't forget to put it in.

1. 65% of the people in a town of 24,000 are over the age of sixteen. How many people are over the age of sixteen?

_____

How many are age sixteen or younger?

_____

2. 4 % of a man's corn crop was destroyed by heavy rains. If the total crop was 8,900 bushels, how much was destroyed?

_____

How much was not destroyed?_____

3. A woman puts $7,800 in a bank and will get 5.3% interest a year. How much interest will she get each year?

_____

4. A school has 900 students. It is 55% white, 35% Black, and 10% Asian.

How many white students are there?

_____

How many Black students are there?

_____

How many Asian students are there?

_____

5. A spelling test had 50 questions. If a girl got 98% right, how many questions did she get right?

_____

How many were wrong? _____

6. In a state with 450,000 people, three candidates were running for governor. Figure out how many votes each one got.

Mario Voteforme, 36% of the vote.

_____

Tina Lawandorder, 22% of the vote.

_____

Joe Prosperity, 42% of the vote.

_____

7. A tank of gasoline is 76% used up. What percent is not used up?

_____

8. A school is 49% boys. What percent is girls?

_____

9. There were three candidates for office. One got 41% of the votes, the second 23%. What percent of the votes did the third candidate get?

_____

Test 30 — Percent

Change the following percents to decimals.

1. 68% = _____

2. 4% = _____

3. 137% = _____

Work out the next three problems.

4. What is 15% of 400?

_____

5. What is 125% of 64?

_____

6. What is 90% of 500?

_____

Now try these word problems.

7. A woman has $4,300 in a bank. How much interest will she get in one year if the bank pays 6% interest?

_____

8. There were 50 questions on a spelling test. A boy got 96% right. How many questions did he get right?

_____

9. 7% of the students in a school failed a test. What percent passed?

_____

10. A class has 30 students. 40% of them are boys. How many girls are there? Be careful. First figure out how many boys there are.

_____

1. Figure out what *A* is on the following number line.

8   A   20

A = _____

2. Write 308,000,000,000 in words.

_____

3. Factor 70 three ways. _____

_____   _____

4. 42465 ÷ 8 = _____

5. Find the average of 9, 14, 25, and 32.

_____

6. Write seventeen and four thousandths in decimals.

_____

7. 69 + 2.637 + 2.18 = _____

8. 2.7 − 1.342 = _____

9. Round off 28,723 to the nearest thousand.

_____

10. Round off .4265943 to the nearest hundredth.

_____

11. .273 × 69 = _____

12. Write MMCDLXXIII in Arabic numbers.

_____

13. 198.36 ÷ 2.9 = _____

14. 5^4 = _____

15. What fraction of the circle is shaded in?

_____

16. If $\dfrac{9}{13}$ of a test is right, what fraction is wrong?

_____

17. Complete the ratio.

6 : 48 = _____ : 56

18. $\dfrac{2}{7} + \dfrac{2}{3}$ = _____

19. Reduce the following fractions to lowest terms.

$\dfrac{9}{8}$ = _____ $\dfrac{12}{16}$ = _____

20. Change $9\dfrac{3}{7}$ to an improper fraction.

_____

21. $5\dfrac{2}{5}$ 22. $9\dfrac{1}{7}$

  $+7\dfrac{4}{5}$ $-4\dfrac{3}{7}$

23. Write point *B* as a mixed number. Reduce your answer to lowest terms.

4   B   5

B = _____

24. $1\dfrac{9}{10}$ of $\dfrac{2}{3}$ = _____

25. $\dfrac{2}{5} ÷ \dfrac{7}{10}$ = _____

26. $\dfrac{1}{3}$ as a percent = _____

75% as a fraction = _____

There are three *dimensions*.

Lines have one dimension. They are called *one-dimensional*.

Flat shapes have two dimensions. They are called *two-dimensional*.

Solid objects have three dimensions. They are called *three-dimensional*.

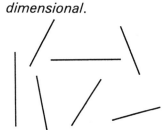
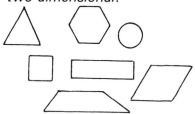
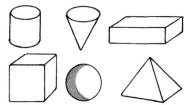

Next to each shape, write how many dimensions it has. Try to remember the names of the shapes — they are all important. Under the name of each shape, make your own small drawing of it.

1. Triangle  —
7. Circle —
13. Rhombus  —

2. Cube —
8. Box —
14. Ellipse  —

3. Cone —
9. Cylinder —
15. Trapezoid —

4. Rectangle —
10. Sphere —
16. Hexagon  —

5. Square —
11. Line —
17. Pentagon 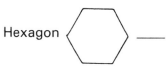 —

6. Pyramid  —
12. Parallelogram —
18. Line 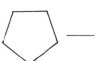 —

After each shape, give examples of that shape in the world around you. Think of as many objects as you can for each shape.

Two-dimensional Shapes

1.  Triangle _____

2. Rectangle _____

3. Square _____

4. Circle _____

5. Parallelogram _____

6. Rhombus _____

7. Ellipse _____

8. Trapezoid _____

9. Pentagon _____

10. Hexagon _____

Three-dimensional Shapes

11.  Pyramid _____

12. Box _____

13. Cube _____

14. Sphere _____

15. Cone _____

16. Cylinder _____

Give the names of the following shapes.

17. _____

18. _____

19. _____

20. _____

21. _____

22. _____

23. _____

1. 50% of 72 = _____

2. 15% of 60 = _____

3. 92% of 980 = _____

4. 7.5% as a decimal = _____

5. 92% as a decimal = _____

6. 120% as a decimal = _____

7. If 48% is right, what percent is wrong?

_____

8. If 99% is finished, what percent is unfinished?

_____

Write the percent equivalent for each fraction below.

9. $\frac{1}{3}$ = _____

10. $\frac{2}{3}$ = _____

11. $\frac{1}{2}$ = _____

12. $\frac{3}{4}$ = _____

13. $\frac{1}{4}$ = _____

14. $\frac{2}{5}$ = _____

15. $\frac{9}{10}$ = _____

Write the fraction equivalent for each percent below.

16. 99% = _____

17. 60% = _____

18. 10% = _____

19. $12\frac{1}{2}$% = _____

20. Use a ruler to measure this line.

_____ = _____

Reduce the following.

21. $\frac{6}{48}$ = _____   22. $\frac{14}{16}$ = _____

23. Write 14.09 in words.

_____

24. Write twelve million in numbers.

_____

25. Write $9\frac{1}{7}$ as an improper fraction.

_____

26. $\frac{8}{15} \div \frac{4}{5}$ = _____

27. $\frac{4}{7} \times \frac{14}{15}$ = _____

28. $\frac{8}{9} + \frac{8}{9}$ = _____

29. $\begin{array}{r} 7\frac{1}{11} \\ -\ 4\frac{3}{11} \\ \hline \end{array}$ 30. $\begin{array}{r} 5\frac{2}{3} \\ +\ 4\frac{2}{3} \\ \hline \end{array}$

31. $\frac{9}{10} - \frac{1}{4}$ = _____

32. $\frac{3}{4} + \frac{1}{7}$ = _____

33. Four cubed = _____

34. 324.544 ÷ .64 = _____

35. Use Roman numerals to write 1,466.

_____

36. 97.1 × 65 = _____

37. Round off 16.9342179 to the nearest thousandth.

_____

38. 69 − 14.691 = _____

39. A new color TV usually costs $418, but it is being sold at a 15% discount. How much is the discount?

_____

40. How much does the TV cost now? _____

41. Manuel's piggy bank had 47 quarters, 211 dimes, 41 nickels, and 150 pennies in it. How much is all that in dollars and cents?

_____

42. How many days are in March? _____

43. How many days are in November? _____

44. How many days are in January? _____

45. How many quarts are in 5 gallons? _____

Give the names of the following shapes. Inside the shape, write the number of dimensions it has.

Example:

 Triangle

1.  _____

2.  _____

3.  _____

4.  _____

5.  _____

6. _____

7. _____

8.  _____

9.  _____

10.  _____

11.  _____

12.  _____

13.  _____

14. 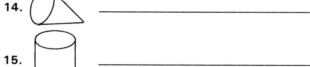 _____

15. _____

Next to the name of each shape, draw a picture of it. Be neat!

16. Pyramid

17. Box

18. Rhombus

19. Square

20. Pentagon
(five sides)

21. Ellipse

22. Sphere

23. Triangle

24. Cube

25. Parallelogram

26. Cylinder

27. Rectangle

28. Circle

29. Trapezoid

30. Cone

31. Hexagon
(six sides)

**Next to each shape below, write its name and the number of dimensions it has.
Choose your answers from this list:**

triangle	parallelogram	pentagon	cube
rectangle	rhombus	hexagon	sphere
square	ellipse	pyramid	cone
circle	trapezoid	box	cylinder

1. _____ _____

2. _____ _____

3. _____ _____

4. _____ _____

5. _____ _____

6. _____ _____

7. _____ _____

8. _____ _____

9. _____ _____

10. _____ _____

11.  _____ _____

12. _____ _____

13. _____ _____

14. _____ _____

15. _____ _____

16. _____ _____

17. What is the shape of a basketball?

_____

18. What is the shape of a can of cola?

_____

19. What is the shape of a brick?

_____

20. What is the shape of a party hat?

_____

Test 31 — Shapes and Dimensions

Next to each shape, write the number of dimensions it has.

1. 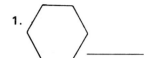 _____

2. _____

3. 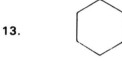 _____

4.  _____

Name the following shapes. Choose your answers from the list below.

cylinder	box	trapezoid	triangle
cone	pyramid	ellipse	rhombus
sphere	hexagon	rectangle	parallelogram
cube	pentagon	circle	square

5.  _____

6. _____

7. _____

8. _____

9.  _____

10. _____

11. _____

12. _____

13. 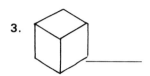 _____

14. 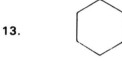 _____

15.  _____

16.  _____

17.  _____

18. 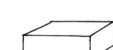 _____

19. _____

20. _____

1. Figure out what *A* is on the following number line.

15   A   45

A = _____

2. Write forty-seven million in numbers.

_____

3. Factor 48 four ways._____   _____

_____   _____

4. $45335 \div 9 =$ _____

5. Find the average of 36, 29, and 43.

_____

6. Write 7.13 in words.

_____

7. $293.774 + 3.6 + 18 =$ _____

8. $29.4 - 1.217 =$ _____

9. Round off 271,435,628 to the nearest million.

_____

10. Round off .477921836 to the nearest thousandth.

_____

11. $7.93 \times .64 =$ _____

12. Write 2,739 in Roman numerals.

_____

13. $23.154 \div .34 =$ _____

14. Five cubed = _____

15. What fraction of the circle is shaded in?

_____

16. If $\frac{7}{11}$ of a race is finished, what fraction is left to go?

_____

17. Complete the ratio.

$9 : 27 = 11 :$ _____

18. $\frac{4}{5} - \frac{3}{8} =$ _____

19. Reduce the following fractions to lowest terms.

$\frac{9}{45} =$ _____ $\frac{4}{22} =$ _____

20. Change $4\frac{7}{8}$ to an improper fraction.

_____

21. $\begin{array}{r} 9\frac{4}{9} \\ +6\frac{7}{9} \\ \hline \end{array}$ 22. $\begin{array}{r} 7\frac{1}{5} \\ -2\frac{4}{5} \\ \hline \end{array}$

23. Write point *B* as a mixed number. Reduce the answer to lowest terms.

2   B   3

B = _____

24. $\frac{4}{9}$ of 27 = _____

25. $\frac{4}{7} \div \frac{20}{21}$ _____

26. $\frac{1}{5}$ as a percent = _____

$66\frac{2}{3}\%$ as a fraction = _____

27. 95% of 200 = _____

28. If 47% of a test is wrong, what percent is right?

_____

Unit 32 — Perimeter 1

The *perimeter* is the distance all the way around the outside of something. To find the perimeter of any shape, add up the lengths of its sides.

Find the perimeters of the following shapes. Mark your answers in feet, inches, or miles.

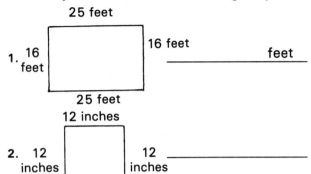

1. 16 feet — 25 feet — 16 feet — 25 feet _____ feet

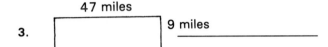

2. 12 inches — 12 inches — 12 inches — 12 inches _____

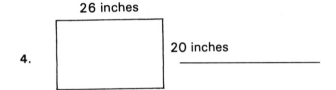

3. 47 miles — 9 miles _____

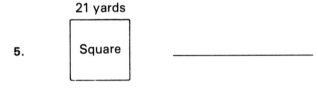

4. 26 inches — 20 inches _____

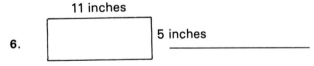

5. 21 yards — Square _____

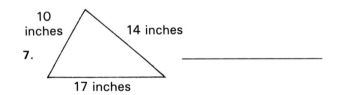

6. 11 inches — 5 inches _____

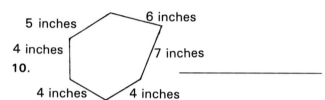

7. 10 inches — 14 inches — 17 inches _____

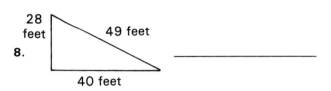

8. 28 feet — 49 feet — 40 feet _____

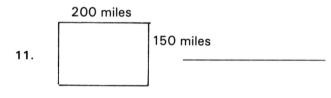

9. 12 inches — 14 inches — 13 inches — 21 inches _____

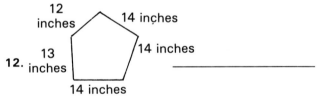

10. 5 inches — 6 inches — 4 inches — 7 inches — 4 inches — 4 inches _____

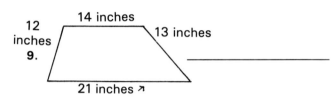

11. 200 miles — 150 miles _____

12. 12 inches — 14 inches — 13 inches — 14 inches — 14 inches _____

13. Each side is 9 feet. _____

Perimeter 2

Remember: the perimeter is the distance all the way around the outside of something.
Find the perimeters of the following shapes. Be sure to mark your answers in inches, feet, miles, or yards.

Rectangle

Square

1. What is the perimeter of a rectangle 15 feet long and 10 feet wide?

_____

2. What is the perimeter of a rectangle 24 inches long and 11 inches wide?

_____

3. What is the perimeter of a rectangle 200 miles long and 150 miles wide?

_____

4. What is the perimeter of a field 50 yards long and 29 yards wide?

_____

5. What is the perimeter of a house 39 feet long and 28 feet wide?

_____

6. What is the perimeter of a room 30 feet long and 22 feet wide?

_____

7. What is the perimeter of a rug 12 feet long and 9 feet wide?

_____

8. What is the perimeter of a square whose sides are each 9 inches long?

_____

9. What is the perimeter of a square whose sides are each 95 yards long?

_____

10. What is the perimeter of a square whose sides are each 47 miles long?

Regular Hexagon

All sides are equal.

11. What is the perimeter of a hexagon whose sides are each 6 inches long?

_____

12. What is the perimeter of a hexagon whose sides are each 49 feet long?

_____

13. What is the perimeter of a hexagon whose sides are each 427 yards long?

_____

After each shape, write its name. Then write the number of dimensions it has.

1. _____ 2. _____

3. _____ 4. _____

5. _____ 6. _____

7. _____ 8. _____

9. _____ 10. _____

11. _____ 12. _____

13. If 63% of the class is boys, what percent is girls?

_____

14. 18% of 650 =_____

15. 80% as a fraction =_____

16. 25% as a fraction =_____

17. $\frac{11}{12} \div \frac{5}{6}$ = _____

18. $\frac{1}{2}$ of 18 = _____

19. $\frac{9}{10} \times \frac{6}{7}$ = _____

20. Use a ruler to measure the line.

_____ =_____

Reduce the following fractions to lowest terms.

21. $\frac{8}{20}$ =_____   22. $\frac{9}{15}$ =_____

23. Write $2\frac{1}{9}$ as an improper fraction.

_____

24. $8\frac{3}{4}$ $+2\frac{1}{4}$ 25. $9\frac{1}{7}$ $-2\frac{6}{7}$

26. $\frac{2}{3} + \frac{1}{6}$ = _____

27. $\frac{3}{4} - \frac{1}{7}$ = _____

28. $7^2 + 9^2$ = _____

29. $111.54 \div .26$ = _____

30. Write MMCDXLIV as an Arabic number.

_____

31. Round off 73.911113 to the nearest one.

_____

32. Round off 56,277 to the nearest thousand.

_____

33. Ms. Rumple drove her car 93,005 miles before it fell to pieces. She said that over the years the car went 19 miles for every gallon of gas. How much gas did the car use in its lifetime?

_____

34. If gas cost an average of $ .81 over the years, how much did Ms. Rumple spend on gas?

_____

35. Helene got $5.00 and gave half of it to her brother. She spent half of what she had left on candy. How much money did she have then?

_____

36. Circle the metric measure you would use to measure the thickness of a nickel.
     millimeter
     centimeter
     meter
     kilometer

37. Which metric measure would you use to measure the length of a pencil?

_____

38. Which metric measure would you use to measure the distance to the moon?

_____

39. How many quarts are in a gallon? _____

40. How many days are in a week? _____

41. How many days are in a leap year? _____

42. How many days are in February in a leap year?

     _____

43. How many years are in a century? _____

44. How many pounds are in 2 tons? _____

45. How many feet are in 2 miles? _____

46. How many inches are in 5 feet? _____

Perimeter 3

Below, there are six shapes which you will be using in the problems on this page. Remember which shape is which!

Rectangle	Square	Triangle	Trapezoid	Regular Hexagon	Pentagon

   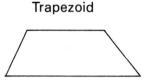

Answer the following questions.

1. What is the perimeter of a rectangle 16 feet long and 11 feet wide?

2. What is the perimeter of a triangle with sides of 5 inches, 3 inches, and 9 inches?

3. What is the perimeter of a square with sides of 52 inches?

4. Each side of a pentagon measures 24 feet. What is the perimeter of the pentagon?

5. What is the perimeter of a triangle with sides of 93 miles, 28 miles, and 22 miles?

6. What is the perimeter of a rectangle 327 yards long and 216 yards wide?

7. Each side of a hexagon measures 71 feet. What is the perimeter of the hexagon?

8. What is the perimeter of a rectangle 91 miles long and 2 miles wide?

9. What is the perimeter of a trapezoid with sides of 8 feet, 9 feet, 11 feet, and 10 feet?

Perimeter 4

Work out the following problems. Make a small drawing of each shape if it will help you.

1. What is the perimeter of a rectangle 19 feet long and 16 feet wide?

   _____

2. What is the perimeter of a triangle whose sides are 12 inches, 10 inches, and 8 inches?

   _____

3. What is the perimeter of a hexagon whose sides are all 15 yards long?

   _____

4. What is the perimeter of a rectangle 325 yards long and 210 yards wide?

   _____

5. What is the perimeter of a pentagon whose sides are all 32 inches long?

   _____

6. What is the perimeter of a trapezoid whose sides are 28 feet, 35 feet, 28 feet, and 19 feet?

   _____

7. What is the perimeter of a rectangle 200 miles long and 15 miles wide?

   _____

8. What is the perimeter of a triangle with sides of 191 yards, 100 yards, and 85 yards?

   _____

9. What is the perimeter of a rectangle 85 miles long and 34 miles wide?

   _____

10. What is the perimeter of a square with sides 84 yards long?

   _____

Work out the following problems.

1. What is the perimeter of a rectangle 35 feet long and 19 feet wide?

2. What is the perimeter of a square whose sides are all 15 yards long?

3. What is the perimeter of a triangle with sides of 43 yards, 23 yards, and 18 yards?

4. What is the perimeter of a hexagon whose sides are all 4 miles long?

5. What is the perimeter of a pentagon whose sides are all 300 yards long?

6. What is the perimeter of a rectangle 341 miles long and 112 miles wide?

7. What is the perimeter of a trapezoid with sides of 32 inches, 21 inches, 14 inches, and 9 inches?

8. What is the perimeter of a square with sides of 98 yards?

9. What is the perimeter of a triangle with sides of 54 yards, 32 yards, and 29 yards?

10. What is the perimeter of a rectangle 465 miles long and 19 miles wide?

1. Figure out what *A* is on the following number line.

   20   A   34

   A = _____

2. Write 907,000,000,000,000 in words.

   _____

3. Factor 56 three ways. _____

   _____   _____

4. 26243 ÷ 8 = _____

5. Find the average of 198 and 134.

   _____

6. Write sixteen and eleven thousandths in decimals.

   _____

7. 180 + 2.73 + 11.9 = _____

8. 61.97 − 4.385 = _____

9. Round off 257,991 to the nearest thousand.

   _____

10. Round off 78.273499 to the nearest one.

    _____

11. 234 × .73 = _____

12. Write MMDCCXLVII as an Arabic number.

    _____

13. 624.96 ÷ 9.3 = _____

14. 4^4 = _____

15. What fraction of the circle is shaded in?

          _____

16. If $\frac{2}{15}$ of a job is done, what fraction remains to be done?

    _____

17. Complete the ratio.

    7 : 49 = _____ : 70

18. $\frac{4}{5} + \frac{1}{8}$ = _____

19. Reduce the following fractions to lowest terms.

    $\frac{7}{42}$ = _____ $\frac{15}{25}$ = _____

20. Change $8\frac{1}{6}$ to an improper fraction.

    _____

21. $7\frac{4}{7}$ 22. $9\frac{1}{3}$

    $+8\frac{5}{7}$ $-4\frac{2}{3}$
    _____   _____

23. Write point *B* as a mixed number. Reduce your answer to lowest terms.

    7   B   8

    B = _____

24. $\frac{7}{8}$ of 40 = _____

25. $\frac{9}{10} \div \frac{11}{15}$ = _____

26. $\frac{1}{3}$ as a percent = _____

    50% as a fraction = _____

27. 82% of 450 = _____

28. If 51% of a school is boys, what percent is girls?

_____

To find the *area* of a rectangle, multiply the length by the width (how long times how wide). The area is how many *square units* there are on a flat surface, so you give the answer in square inches, square feet, square yards, or square miles.

Use the rule stated above to find the answers to the following problems.

1. Find the area of this box. Use the rule you just learned to figure out the answer. Don't count all the square inches!

25 inches

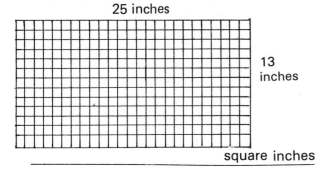

13 inches

_____ square inches

2. What is the area of this box?

15 feet

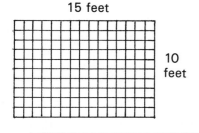

10 feet

_____

3. What is the area of this box?

30 yards

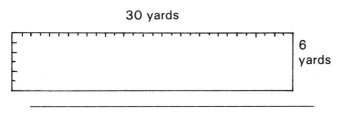

6 yards

_____

4. What is the area of this box?

14 miles

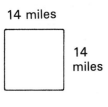

14 miles

_____

5. What is the area of a room 9 feet long and 8 feet wide?

_____

6. What is the area of a field 100 yards long and 50 yards wide?

_____

7. What is the area of a tabletop 18 inches long and 11 inches wide?

_____

8. What is the area of a rectangular city 43 miles long and 16 miles wide?

_____

9. What is the area of a piece of paper 11 inches long and 8 inches wide?

_____

10. What is the area of a playground 40 yards long and 25 yards wide?

_____

11. If you found the area of a piece of note-book paper, would your answer be in square feet, square inches, square yards, or square miles?

_____

12. If you found the area of a basketball court, would your answer be in square inches, square yards, or square miles?

_____

Area and Volume 2

Find the area in the following problems.
Remember: multiply the length by the width and give the answer in square inches, square feet, square yards, or square miles.

1. What is the area of a rug 12 feet long and 9 feet wide?

    _____ square feet

2. What is the area of a roof 15 yards long and 12 yards wide?

    _____

3. What is the area of a field 160 yards long and 92 yards wide?

    _____

4. What is the area of a piece of paper 18 inches long and 6 inches wide?

    _____

5. What is the area of a gymnasium floor 82 yards long and 40 yards wide?

    _____

6. What is the area of a room 22 feet long and 15 feet wide?

    _____

7. A man wants to put new tile on the floor of a room. Each tile is one square foot. How many tiles will he need if the room is 9 feet long and 8 feet wide?

    _____

Find the *volume* in the following problems.
To find the *volume*, multiply the length by the width by the height (or depth).

The *volume* of a solid object or space is the number of *cubic units* in it, so give your answers in cubic inches, cubic feet, cubic yards, or cubic miles.

8. How many cubic inches are there in this box?

    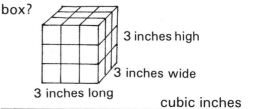

    3 inches high
    3 inches wide
    3 inches long

    _____ cubic inches

9. How many cubic feet are there in this box?

    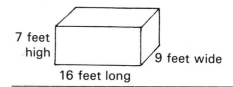

    7 feet high
    9 feet wide
    16 feet long

    _____

10. What is the volume of a box 4 yards long, 3 yards wide, and 2 yards high?

    _____

11. What is the volume of a room 12 feet long, 9 feet wide, and 8 feet high?

    _____

12. What is the volume of a stick of butter 4 inches long, 1 inch wide, and 1 inch high?

    _____

13. If you found the area of a small bedroom, would your answer be in square inches, square feet, or square miles?

    _____

14. If you found the volume of the planet earth, would you state your answer in cubic inches, cubic feet, cubic yards, or cubic miles?

    _____

1. What is the perimeter of a square whose sides are 15 feet long?

   _____

2. What is the perimeter of a basketball court 20 yards long and 12 yards wide?

   _____

3. What is the perimeter of a garden 24 yards long and 13 yards wide?

   _____

Name each shape below.

4.    _____

5.    _____

6.    _____

7.   _____

8. If 29% of the group is men, what percent is women?

   _____

9. 65% of 240 = _____

10. Use a ruler to measure the line.

    _____ = _____

11. 20% as a fraction = _____

12. $\frac{1}{3}$ as a percent = _____

13. $\frac{4}{5} \div \frac{17}{20} =$ _____

14. $\frac{9}{10} \times \frac{5}{6} =$ _____

15. $\frac{3}{4} - \frac{1}{7} =$ _____

16. $\frac{4}{5} + \frac{3}{4} =$ _____

Reduce the following fractions to lowest terms.

17. $\frac{9}{27} =$ _____

18. $\frac{18}{24} =$ _____

19. Write $5\frac{3}{8}$ as an improper fraction.

    _____

20. $8\frac{1}{9}$
    $+7\frac{8}{9}$
    _____

21. $3\frac{1}{3}$
    $-1\frac{2}{3}$
    _____

22. $4^3 =$ _____

23. Two to the fifth = _____

24. $390.83 \div 1.9 =$ _____

25. $16.8 - 14.913 =$ _____

26. Round off .9648371 to the nearest hundredth.

    _____

27. How many days are in April? _____

28. How many days are in July? _____

29. How many days are in December? _____

30. How many days are in February? _____

31. How many feet are in a mile? _____

32. How many inches are in a foot? _____

33. How many feet are in a yard? _____

34. How many pints are in a quart? _____

35. How many cents are in a half-dollar?

    _____

36. How many nickels are in a dollar? _____

37. How many minutes are in an hour? _____

38. Circle the metric measure you would use to measure the height of a house.
      millimeters
      centimeters
      meters
      kilometers

39. Circle the metric measure you would use to measure the amount of water in a swimming pool.
      milliliter
      liter

40. A car weighs 3,980 pounds. $\frac{1}{5}$ of the weight of the car is the engine. How much does the engine weigh?

    _____

41. If 7 men divide up $3,000 so each gets the same amount, how much does each man get?

    _____

    How much is left over?

    _____

42. Carlos earns $118.35 each day. How much does he make in 24 days?

    _____

Find the area in the following problems. Remember to give the answers in *square* units.

1. What is the area of a room 16 feet long and 9 feet wide?

_____

2. What is the area of a rug 9 feet long and 7 feet wide?

_____

3. What is the area of a lawn 16 yards long and 12 yards wide?

_____

4. What is the area of a field 24 yards long and 17 yards wide?

_____

5. What is the area of a piece of paper 6 inches long and 5 inches wide?

_____

6. What is the area of a tabletop 18 inches long and 14 inches wide?

_____

7. What is the area of a room 22 feet long and 19 feet wide?

_____

Find the volume in the following problems. Remember to give the answers in *cubic* units.

8. What is the volume of a shoe box 12 inches long, 5 inches wide, and 4 inches deep?

_____

9. What is the volume of a grave 6 feet long, 3 feet wide, and 6 feet deep?

_____

10. What is the volume of a room 10 feet long, 9 feet wide, and 8 feet high?

_____

11. What is the volume of a prison cell 8 feet long, 8 feet wide, and 7 feet high?

_____

12. What is the volume of a desk drawer 14 inches long, 13 inches wide, and 5 inches deep?

_____

13. What is the volume of a box 8 feet long, 8 feet wide, and 8 feet high?

_____

Area and Volume 4

Find the area or volume in the following problems. Remember to give the answers in square units or in cubic units.

1. What is the area of a piece of paper 17 inches long and 11 inches wide?

   _____

2. What is the area of a floor 19 yards long and 16 yards wide?

   _____

3. What is the volume of a box 14 inches long, 12 inches wide, and 4 inches deep?

   _____

4. What is the volume of a hole in the ground 26 yards long, 21 yards wide, and 16 yards deep?

   _____

5. What is the area of a field 180 feet long and 97 feet wide?

   _____

6. What is the volume of a box 4 inches long, 4 inches wide, and 3 inches high?

   _____

7. What is the volume of a room 10 yards long, 7 yards wide, and 4 yards high?

   _____

8. What is the area of a tabletop 21 inches long and 14 inches wide?

   _____

9. What is the area of a land area 47 miles long and 25 miles wide?

   _____

Work out the following problems.

1. What is the area of a football field 100 yards long and 50 yards wide?

2. What is the volume of a box 4 feet long, 3 feet wide, and 7 feet deep?

3. What is the volume of a room 10 feet long, 9 feet wide, and 7 feet high?

4. What is the area of a piece of paper 8 inches long and 11 inches wide?

5. What is the volume of a book 4 inches long, 4 inches wide, and 1 inch high?

6. What is the area of a piece of land 15 miles long and 12 miles wide?

7. What is the volume of a closet 5 feet long, 4 feet wide, and 9 feet high?

8. What is the area of a room's floor that is 67 feet long and 40 feet wide?

9. What is the volume of the inside of a barn that is 47 feet long, 38 feet wide, and 20 feet high?

10. What is the area of a tabletop 35 inches long and 20 inches wide?

1. Figure out what *A* is on the following number line.

   35   A   65

   A = _____

2. Write nine hundred seventy billion in numbers.

   _____

3. Factor 40 three ways. _____

   _____   _____

4. 42260 ÷ 7 = _____

5. Find the average of 99, 87, 22, and 32.

   _____

6. Write 3.05 in words.

   _____

7. 14.93 + 8.291 + 493 = _____

8. 68.4 − 2.97 = _____

9. Round off 888,888,888 to the nearest million.

   _____

10. Round off 29.347921 to the nearest tenth.

    _____

11. .459 × .38 = _____

12. Write 3,955 in Roman numerals.

    _____

13. 259.54 ÷ .38 = _____

14. Eight cubed = _____

15. What fraction of the square is shaded in?

            _____

16. If $\dfrac{14}{21}$ of a test is right, what fraction is wrong?

    _____

17. Complete the ratio.

    8 : 64 = 9 : _____

18. $\dfrac{7}{8} - \dfrac{2}{3} =$ _____

19. Reduce the following fractions to lowest terms.

    $\dfrac{4}{26} =$ _____ $\dfrac{8}{12} =$ _____

20. Change $7\dfrac{2}{3}$ to an improper fraction.

    _____

21. $\begin{array}{r} 4\dfrac{5}{11} \\ +3\dfrac{8}{11} \\ \hline \end{array}$ 22. $\begin{array}{r} 12\dfrac{1}{7} \\ -1\dfrac{5}{7} \\ \hline \end{array}$

23. Write point *B* as a mixed number. Reduce your answer to lowest terms.

    6   B   7

    B = _____

24. $2\dfrac{4}{7} \times \dfrac{7}{8} =$ _____

25. $\dfrac{5}{24} \div \dfrac{7}{8} =$ _____

26. $\dfrac{4}{5}$ as a percent = _____

    $33\dfrac{1}{3}\%$ as a fraction = _____

27. 92% of 150 = _____

28. If 24% of a test is wrong, what percent is right?

_____

29. What is the perimeter of a rectangle 7 miles long and 6 miles wide?

_____

Learn the names of the following terms used with circles.

Circumference	Diameter	Radius	Chord	Tangent	Arc	Semicircle

Now answer the following questions.

1. Which line touches only the outside of the circle? _____

2. Which line goes from the center of the circle to the edge? _____

3. Which line touches the edge of the circle in two places but does not go through the center?

   _____

4. What do you call the distance around the circle? _____

5. What do you call half a circle? _____

6. What do you call a small part of the circumference? _____

7. What do you call the line that cuts the circle in two? _____

If you know the diameter of a circle, you can find the *circumference* by multiplying the diameter by 3.14. This is a special number called *pi*, discovered many years ago. It is from the Greek letter π. You should remember that $\pi = 3.14$.

Work out the following problems on circumference.

8. What is the circumference of a circle whose diameter is 5 inches?

   _____

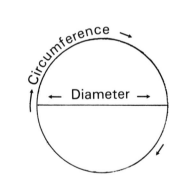

9. What is the circumference of a circle whose diameter is 3 feet?

   _____

10. What is the circumference of a circle whose diameter is 25 miles?

    _____

11. What is the circumference of a circle whose diameter is 65 yards?

    _____

Circumference and Area of the Circle 2

Remember the following terms used with circles.

Circumference   Diameter   Radius   Chord   Tangent   Arc   Semicircle

Using the diagram to the right, find the letters and write the terms which are used with the circle. For example, the term for *AC* on the diagram (the line between *A* and *C*) is *radius*.

1. *AD* _____

2. *BE* _____

3. *FEG* _____

4. *CAE* _____

5. *AB* _____

6. *BC* _____

7. *BCDEB* _____

8. *EDC* _____

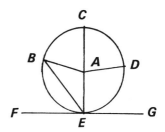

To find the *area* of a circle, use this formula: Area = πr².
This means you should multiply the radius by
itself, and multiply the answer by *pi* (π) or
3.14. Give the answer in square units.

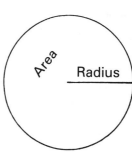

Work out the following problems. You've been given a little help with the first one.

9. What is the area of a circle whose radius is 5 inches?

    Area = πr² = 3.14 × 5² = 3.14 × 25 = _____ square inches

10. What is the area of a circle whose radius is 3 feet?

_____

11. What is the area of a city whose radius is 8 miles?

_____

Label each of the following as inches, square inches, or cubic inches.

1. Area of a table _____

2. Volume of a shoe box _____

3. Perimeter of a paper _____

4. Area of a paper _____

5. Volume of an engine _____

6. Perimeter of a table _____

7. What is the perimeter of a room 27 feet long and 26 feet wide?

_____

8. If 29% of a group is male, what percent is female?

_____

9. 89% of 2,400 = _____

10. $\frac{7}{10}$ as a percent = _____

11. 75% as a fraction = _____

12. $\frac{7}{8} \times \frac{4}{5} =$ _____

13. $\frac{2}{3}$ of 39 = _____

14. $\frac{3}{4} \div \frac{7}{8} =$ _____

15. Use a ruler to measure the line.

_____ = ____

Reduce the following fractions to lowest terms.

16. $\frac{9}{12} =$ ____   17. $\frac{15}{45} =$ ____

18. $7\frac{3}{11}$
   $+9\frac{9}{11}$

19. $9\frac{1}{7}$
   $-1\frac{4}{7}$

20. Round off 4.743992 to the nearest hundredth.

_____

21. Write $7\frac{3}{5}$ as an improper fraction.

_____

22. $2^5 =$ _____

23. $\frac{3}{5} + \frac{4}{5} =$ _____

24. $\frac{7}{8} - \frac{2}{3} =$ _____

25. $\frac{5}{7} + \frac{1}{2} =$ _____

26. 78.728 ÷ .26 = _____

27. Write MCDLXIV as an Arabic number.

_____

28. 47.9 + 2.73 + 90 = _____

29. 14.8 − 7.219 = _____

How many dimensions does each of the following shapes have?

30.  ____   33. ⬭ ____

31.  ____   34. 🌀 ____

32. ▭ ____   35. ⬭ ____

126

36. _____

38. _____

37 _____

39. Circle the metric measure which is closest to a mile.

millimeter

centimeter

meter

kilometer

40. Circle the metric measure which is closest to a pound.

milligram

gram

kilogram

41. Which metric measure would you use to measure a football field?

_____

42. Which metric measure would you use to measure the milk on a milk truck?

_____

43. How many years are in a century? _____

44. How many cups are in a pint? _____

45. How many inches are in a foot? _____

46. How many seconds are in a minute? _____

47. How many hours are in a day? _____

48. Hamburger meat costs $1.95 a pound. How much would it cost a restaurant to buy a ton of hamburger meat?

_____

49. Mr. Spache has $1,218.43 in his savings account. He puts in $531 in May, $117.21 in June, and $219.11 in July. Then in August he takes out $900 to pay for a plane ticket to Europe. How much is left in his account?

_____

Remember the following terms used with the circle.

Circumference	Distance around the circle
Diameter	Line cutting the circle in two
Radius	Line from the center to the edge
Tangent	Line touching only the outside of the circle
Arc	A small part of the circumference
Semicircle	Half a circle
Chord	Line touching the edge of the circle in two places but not going through the center

Using the diagram to the right, find the letters and write the terms which are used with the circle.

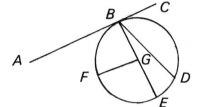

Example: *GF* = Radius

1. *BG* _____

2. *BD* _____

3. *BDEFB* _____

4. *ABC* _____

5. *EG* _____

6. *BGE* _____

7. *DE* _____

8. *BDE* _____

9. *BFE* _____

On each circle below, make a drawing to show that you understand the term written above the circle.

10. Circumference 11. Tangent 12. Semicircle 13. Radius 14. Arc 15. Chord 16. Diameter

17. What is the number you multiply by the diameter to get the circumference?

_____ (pi or π)
If you don't know this number, learn it!

18. What is the circumference of a circle whose diameter is 7 inches?

_____

19. What is the circumference of a circle whose diameter is 9 miles?

_____

20. What is the circumference of a circle whose diameter is 32 yards?

_____

21. What is the area of a round swimming pool whose radius is 7 yards?

_____

22. What is the area of a frying pan whose radius is 5 inches?

_____

23. What is the area of a circle whose radius is 2 miles?

_____

24. What is the area of a circle whose radius is 1 foot?

_____

Circumference and Area of the Circle 4

On the line, write the term that goes with each group of letters. Choose your answers from the list next to the drawing.

1. *EFG*_____

2. *FD* _____

3. *BEC*_____

4. *FG* _____

5. *DG* _____

6. *GDE* _____

7. *ADC* _____

8. *DE* _____

9. *FE* _____

10. *GDEG*_____

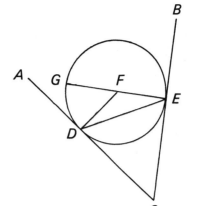

Circumference
Diameter
Radius
Chord
Tangent
Arc
Semicircle

Remember two important formulas:

Circumference = πd

Area = πr² (square units)

Use these formulas to figure out the following problems.

11. What is the area of a circle whose radius is 5 feet?

_____ square feet

12. What is the circumference of a circle whose diameter is 32 inches?

_____ inches

13. What is the circumference of a field whose diameter is 450 feet?

_____

14. What is the area of a circle whose radius is 4 miles?

_____

15. What is the area of a circle whose radius is 10 feet?

_____

16. What is the circumference of a circle whose diameter is 19 yards?

_____

17. What is the area of a circle whose radius is 12 miles?

_____

On the line, write the term that goes with each group of letters. Choose your answers from the list next to the drawing.

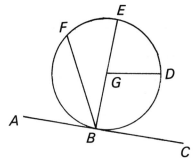

Circumference
Diameter
Radius
Chord
Tangent
Arc
Semicircle

1. *FE* _____

2. *GD* _____

3. *BF* _____

4. *ABC* _____

5. *BGE* _____

6. *BDEFB* _____

7. *BDE* _____

Work out the following problems.

8. What is the circumference of a circle whose diameter is 3 inches?

_____

9. What is the circumference of a circle whose diameter is 6 miles?

_____

10. What is the circumference of a circle whose diameter is 8 yards?

_____

11. What is the circumference of a circle whose radius is 2 inches?

_____

12. What is the area of a circle whose radius is 4 miles?

_____

13. What is the area of a circle whose radius is 2 feet?

_____

14. What is the area of a circle whose radius is 9 yards?

_____

15. What is the area of a circle whose radius is 1 inch?

_____

1. Figure out what *A* is on the following number line.

    18   A   63

    A =_____

2. Write 900,000,000 in words.

    _____

3. Factor 30 three ways. _____

    _____   _____

4. 75065 ÷ 9 = _____

5. Find the average of 36, 44, and 52.

    _____

6. Write fifteen and three thousandths in decimals.

    _____

7. 8 + 9.3 + 16.702 = _____

8. 68.59 − 2.473 = _____

9. Round off 278,522 to the nearest thousand.

    _____

10. Round off .4283759 to the nearest hundredth.

    _____

11. 3.75 × 2.9 = _____

12. Write CMXLIV as an Arabic number.

    _____

13. 435.84 ÷ 6.4 = _____

14. 9^2 = _____

15. What fraction of the circle is shaded in?

         _____

16. If $\frac{11}{47}$ of a group of teachers is men, what fraction is women?

    _____

17. Complete the ratio.

    7 : 35 = _____ : 45

18. $\frac{3}{4}$ + $\frac{1}{7}$ = _____

19. Reduce the following fractions to lowest terms.

    $\frac{7}{63}$ = _____ $\frac{32}{40}$ = _____

20. Change $2\frac{9}{10}$ to an improper fraction.

    _____

21. $9\frac{4}{5}$
    $+8\frac{3}{5}$
    _____

22. $2\frac{1}{7}$
    $-1\frac{4}{7}$
    _____

23. Write point *B* as a mixed number. Reduce your answer to lowest terms.

    3   B   4

    B =_____

24. $\frac{7}{9}$ of 81 = _____

25. $\frac{9}{10}$ ÷ $1\frac{3}{4}$ = _____

26. $\frac{1}{2}$ as a percent = _____

    75% as a fraction = _____

27. 35% of 240 = _____

28. If 18% of a group is male, what percent is female?

_____

29. What is the perimeter of a rectangle 14 miles long and 10 miles wide?

_____

30. What is the area of the rectangle in question 29?

_____

31. What is the volume of a box 8 inches long, 4 inches wide, and 2 inches high?

_____

Unit 35 — Different Bases 1

Our number system is called *base ten* because there are ten different single numbers: 0, 1, 2, 3, 4, 5, 6, 7, 8, and 9. The way we can count higher than 9 is by putting numbers in different places, as in the tens or the hundreds or the millions place.

But base ten isn't the only way to write numbers. We use it mainly because we have ten fingers. What if we had only eight fingers? Or seven? It is possible to write numbers in base eight or base seven or any other base.

Count the Xs in each line below. Then figure out the number of Xs in each base. The first one has been done for you.

	Base Ten		Base Eight		Base Seven	
	groups of ten ↓	ones left over ↓	groups of eight ↓	ones left over ↓	groups of seven ↓	ones left over ↓
XXXXXXXXXXXX	1	2	1	4	1	5
1. XXXXXXXXXXXXXXXXX						
2. XXXXXXXXXX						
3. XXXXXXXX						
4. XXXXXX						
5. XXXXXXXXXXXXXXXXXXXXXX						
6. XXXXXXXXXXXXXX						
7. XXXXXXXXXXXXXXXXXXXXXXXXXX						
8. XXXX						
9. XXXXXXXX						
10. XXXXXXXXXXXXXXXXXXXXXXXXXXXXXX XX						
11. XXXXXXXXXXXXXXXXXXXXXXXXXXXXX XXXX						
12. XXXXXXXXXXX						
13. XXXXXXXXXXXXXXXXXXXXXXXXXXXXXX XXXXXX						

133

For each line below, figure out the number of *X*s in each base. You will have to count the number of *X*s in each line.

	Base Ten		Base Five		Base Eight	
	groups of ten ↓	ones ↓	groups of five ↓	ones ↓	groups of eight ↓	ones ↓
XXXXXXXXXX	1	1	2	1	1	3
1. XXXXX						
2. XXXXXXXXXXXXXX						
3. XXXXXXXXXXXXXXXXXX						
4. XXXXXXXXXXXXXX						
5. XXXXXXXXXXXXXXXXXXXX						
6. XXXXXXXXXXXXXXXXXXXXXX						
7. XXXXXXXXXXXXXXXXXXXXXXXX						
8. XXXXXXX						
9. XXXXXXXXXXXXXXXXXXXXXXXXXXXXXXX						
10. XX						

The numbers below are given in base six or base nine. Change them to base ten (our number system). Study the examples first.

Base Six   **Base Ten**

sixes ones

  2   3 = $(2 \times 6) + 3 =$ 15

11. 1   4 = $(1 \times 6) + 4 =$

12. 3   5 =

13. 2   1 =

14. 1   1 =

15. 5   5 =

16. 2   4 =

Base Nine   **Base Ten**

nines ones

  2   3 = $(2 \times 9) + 3 =$ 21

17. 1   4 =

18. 3   5 =

19. 6   1 =

20. 4   3 =

21. 8   8 =

22. 1   1 =

1. 1207 × 427 = _____

2. What is the area of a circle whose radius is 2 miles?

_____

3. What is the area of a rectangle 17 feet long and 8 feet wide?

_____

4. What is the circumference of a circle whose diameter is 9 yards?

_____

5. What is the volume of a box 3 inches long, 3 inches wide, and 2 inches high?

_____

6. What is the perimeter of a hexagon whose sides are all 7 inches long?

_____

7. If 77% of the rooms in a hotel are full, what percent are empty?

_____

8. 25% of 96 = _____

9. $\frac{2}{5}$ as a percent = _____

10. 80% written as a fraction = _____

11. 54.162 ÷ .18 = _____

12. Measure the line.

_____ = _____

13. $\frac{7}{8}$ of 72 = _____

14. $\frac{2}{3} \div \frac{7}{9}$ = _____

15. $\frac{7}{11} \times \frac{4}{21}$ = _____

16. $7\frac{4}{5}$
    $+9\frac{1}{5}$
    _____

17. $9\frac{1}{3}$
    $-1\frac{2}{3}$
    _____

18. Round off 69.51137 to the nearest one.

_____

19. Write $2\frac{7}{8}$ as an improper fraction.

_____

Reduce the following fractions to lowest terms.

20. $\frac{6}{36}$ = _____

21. $\frac{4}{50}$ = _____

22. $10^2 + 5^3$ = _____

23. Write 1,551 in Roman numerals.

_____

24. 147.9 + 8.3 + 1 = _____

25. 16 − .37 = _____

Identify the following shapes by name.

26. _____

27. _____

28. _____

29. _____

30. _____

31.  _____

32. How many days are in January? _____

33. How many days are in June? _____

34. How many days are in September? _____

35. How many days are in November? _____

36. How many feet are in a mile? _____

37. How many days are in a non-leap year?

_____

38. How many ounces are in a pound? _____

39. How many quarts are in a gallon? _____

40. How many years are in a decade? _____

41. How many pounds are in a ton? _____

42. Circle the metric measure which is closest to a mile.

meter

centimeter

kilometer

millimeter

43. Circle the metric measure which is closest to a quart.

milliliter

liter

44. Mr. Small, a farmer, decided to walk all the way around the outside of a large field on his farm to check the fence for holes. If the field was 285 yards long and 116 yards wide, how far did he walk?

_____

45. How many feet is that? _____

Different Bases 3

For each line below, figure out the number of *X*s in each base.

	Base Ten		Base Nine		Base Eleven	
	tens	ones	nines	ones	elevens	ones
1. XXXXXXXXXXX						
2. XXXXXXXXXXXXX						
3. XXXXX						
4. XXXXXXXXXXXXXXXXX						
5. XXXXXXXXXXXXX						
6. XXX						
7. XXXXXXXXXXXXXXXXXXXXX						
8. XXXXXXXXXXXXXXXXXXXXX						
9. XXXXXXXXXXXXXXXXXXXXXXXXXXXXXXXX						
10. XXXXXXXXXXXXXXXXXX						
11. XXXXXXXX						

The numbers below are given in bases different from our number system. Change these numbers to base-ten numbers (our system).

Base Five		Base Ten		Base Seven		Base Ten		Base Eleven		Base Ten
fives	ones			sevens	ones			elevens	ones	
12. 2	4	= _____	17.	1	6	= _____	22.	9	4	= _____
13. 3	1	= _____	18.	2	1	= _____	23.	6	1	= _____
14. 4	3	= _____	19.	3	5	= _____	24.	2	3	= _____
15. 1	0	= _____	20.	5	6	= _____	25.	2	0	= _____
16. 3	4	= _____	21.	3	0	= _____	26.	8	3	= _____

Below are base-ten numbers. Write them as base-six, base-eight, and base-eleven numbers.

Base Ten		Base Six		Base Eight		Base Eleven	
tens	ones	sixes	ones	eights	ones	elevens	ones
1. 1	5	_____		_____		_____	
2. 2	5	_____		_____		_____	
3.	6	_____		_____		_____	
4. 3	5	_____		_____		_____	
5. 2	2	_____		_____		_____	

The numbers below are written in different bases. Change them all to base-ten numbers.

Base Seven		Base Ten		Base Four		Base Ten		Base Five		Base Ten
6. 1 6	=	_____		**12.** 3 1	=	_____		**18.** 4 2	=	_____
7. 2 4	=	_____		**13.** 1 3	=	_____		**19.** 1 4	=	_____
8. 4 6	=	_____		**14.** 2 2	=	_____		**20.** 2 0	=	_____
9. 2 0	=	_____		**15.** 3 0	=	_____		**21.** 4 4	=	_____
10. 1 1	=	_____		**16.** 1 1	=	_____		**22.** 1 1	=	_____
11. 3 3	=	_____		**17.** 3 2	=	_____		**23.** 3 3	=	_____

Below are base-ten numbers. Write them as base-seven, base-eight, and base-five numbers.

	Base Ten	Base Seven	Base Eight	Base Five
1.	22	_____	_____	_____
2.	16	_____	_____	_____
3.	8	_____	_____	_____
4.	11	_____	_____	_____

The numbers below are written in different bases. Change them all to base-ten numbers.

Base Six	Base Ten	Base Three	Base Ten	Base Eleven	Base Ten
5. 54 =	_____	8. 12 =	_____	11. 71 =	_____
6. 12 =	_____	9. 22 =	_____	12. 98 =	_____
7. 33 =	_____	10. 10 =	_____		

1. Figure out what *A* is on the following number line.

10   *A*   70

A = _____

2. Write nine hundred eight trillion in numbers.

_____

3. Factor 24 three ways. _____

_____   _____

4. 42611 ÷ 7 = _____

5. Find the average of 18, 23, and 40.

_____

6. Write 17.012 in words.

_____

7. 144 + 8.38 + 22.105 = _____

8. 22.9 − 4.733 = _____

9. Round off 67,288,920 to the nearest million.

_____

10. Round off 16.93758264 to the nearest thousandth.

_____

11. .289 × 47 = _____

12. Write 2,847 in Roman numerals.

_____

13. 24.447 ÷ .29 = _____

14. Five cubed = _____

15. What fraction of the circle is shaded in?

 _____

16. If $\dfrac{15}{19}$ of a house is painted, what fraction remains to be painted?

_____

17. Complete the ratio.

8 : 96 = 7 : _____

18. $\dfrac{2}{3} - \dfrac{3}{5}$ = _____

19. Reduce the following fractions to lowest terms.

$\dfrac{6}{42}$ = _____ $\dfrac{18}{21}$ = _____

20. Change $9\dfrac{1}{2}$ to an improper fraction.

_____

21. $\begin{array}{r} 5\dfrac{4}{5} \\ +\,4\dfrac{3}{5} \\ \hline \end{array}$

22. $\begin{array}{r} 9\dfrac{1}{3} \\ -\,4\dfrac{2}{3} \\ \hline \end{array}$

23. Write point *B* as a mixed number. Reduce your answer to lowest terms.

7   *B*   8

B = _____

24. $\dfrac{2}{3} \times 1\dfrac{9}{10}$ = _____

25. $\dfrac{4}{5} \div \dfrac{8}{9}$ = _____

26. $\dfrac{3}{8}$ as a percent = _____

$66\dfrac{2}{3}$ % as a fraction = _____

27. 25% of 740 = _____

28. If 63% of a job is done, what percent remains to be done?

_____

29. What is the perimeter of a rectangle 19 miles long and 7 miles wide?

_____

30. What is the area of a rectangle 5 inches long and 4 inches wide?

_____

31. What is the volume of a box 14 feet long, 10 feet wide, and 6 feet high?

_____

32. What is the circumference of a circle whose diameter is 7 feet?

_____

33. What is the area of a circle whose radius is 4 inches?

_____

1. Figure out what *B* is on the following number line.

```
14                   B    42
 |     |     |        |    |
```

B = _____

2. Write 371,000,000,000 in words.

_____

_____

3. Factor 63 two ways. _____

_____

4. 16525 ÷ 8 = _____

5. Find the average of 8, 25, and 12.

_____

6. Write 7.009 in words.

_____

_____

Write twelve and fifteen hundredths in decimals.

_____

7. 45.762 + 396 = _____

8. 6.8 − 2.472 = _____

9. Round off 45,632 to the nearest thousand.

_____

10. Round off .6749831 to the nearest hundredth.

_____

11. 43.7 × 3.9 = _____

12. Write MMCCLXVII in Arabic numbers.

_____

Write 3,424 in Roman numerals.

_____

13. 11.388 ÷ 2.6 = _____

14. Five cubed + nine squared = _____

4^5 = _____

15. What fraction of the circle is shaded in?

_____

16. If $\dfrac{9}{10}$ of a test is right, what fraction is wrong?

_____

17. Complete the ratios.

6 : 18 = 8 : _____

3 : 12 = _____ : 16

18. $\dfrac{2}{3} + \dfrac{1}{4}$ = _____

19. Reduce the following fractions to lowest terms.

$\dfrac{4}{24}$ = _____ $\dfrac{14}{16}$ = _____

20. Write $4\dfrac{1}{8}$ as an improper fraction.

_____

21. $\begin{array}{r} 4\frac{2}{3} \\ +8\frac{2}{3} \\ \hline \end{array}$

22. $\begin{array}{r} 5\frac{1}{5} \\ -2\frac{4}{5} \\ \hline \end{array}$

23. Write point *A* as a mixed number.
Reduce your answer to lowest terms.

3   A   4

A = _____

24. $2\frac{4}{5} \times 1\frac{5}{8} =$ _____

25. $\frac{1}{7} \div \frac{3}{14} =$ _____

26. $\frac{1}{4}$ as a percent = _____

$33\frac{1}{3}$ % as a fraction = _____

27. 45% of 640 = _____

28. If 53% of a school is boys, what percent is girls?

_____

29. What is the perimeter of a rectangular garden 19 feet long and 14 feet wide?

_____

30. What is the area of the garden in question 29?

_____

31. What is the volume of a box 5 feet long, 5 feet wide, and 4 feet deep?

_____

32. What is the circumference of a circle whose diameter is 8 feet?

_____

33. What is the area of a circle whose radius is 3 inches?

_____

Review Test Progress Graph

After each Review Test is corrected, make a bar graph by filling in the number of questions you got right. The top line climbing up the graph is the number of questions on each test, so if you touch the line, you got one hundred percent correct. The lower line climbing up the graph indicates eighty percent correct or the mastery level which you should reach. During the year, you'll be able to see your progress in math.

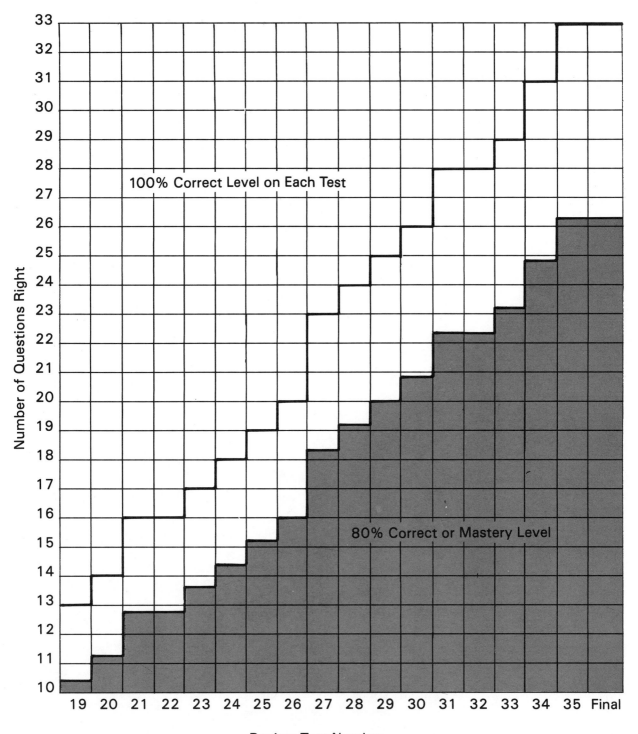

Number of Questions Right

Review Test Number